CW00543567

Praise for *All Peace ...*

"Every now and then you expe... you just love being around, and feel good when you are with them. It is this kind of person you want to learn from because they walk the talk. Jackie Lora Jones is that person, and she gives us an eye-opening look into how we can remember the truth of our nature as Spirit by undoing our illusory perceptions that keep us stuck in ego; our illusory self. Quite frankly, this book will help heal your mind, and assist you in awakening from the dream of separation. It is enlightening and refreshingly uncompromising in its approach. You will further yourself on the spiritual path by reading this book!"

— **Cindy Lora-Renard**, spiritual life coach, international speaker on ACIM and author of *A Course in Health and Well-Being*

"With crystal clarity *All Piece No Pieces* by Jackie Lora Jones brilliantly introduces new readers to the pure non-dual metaphysical masterpiece, *A Course in Miracles*, and provides existing students an excellent opportunity to hone their understanding and practice of its profoundly helpful principles and insights. The writing is engaging and friendly while sticking to the important precepts of the Course without compromise. Highly recommended for both newbie and seasoned Course students!"

— **Bruce Rawles**, author of *The Geometry Code* and ACIMBlog.com

"Dedicated, faithful, entertaining, and knowledgeable, Jackie Lora Jones shows what great benefits the teachings of *A Course in Miracles* have had on her life and in turn can have on your life too."

— **Alexander Marchand**, author/artist of
The Universe Is a Dream

"This spiritual book by Jackie Lora Jones is not only well written, but is totally uncompromising on its message about the spiritual masterpiece this book is about, *A Course in Miracles.* Jackie not only shares many of the Course's definitive, hardcore statements in proper context, but discusses how to achieve, in a very practical way, the goal the aforementioned Course book offers which is done through a non-traditional form of forgiveness also known as *true* forgiveness. Jackie says, 'You can practice true forgiveness in any job, at any place, and at any time. It is not our function to point out the ego in others and police the universe. It is our job to wake up from our dream that there *is* a universe.'

Additionally, the classic film, *The Wizard of Oz,* is used throughout the book as a great analogy for this whole predicament we seem to find ourselves in. There's no place like home, indeed. Giddy up!"

— **Mike Lemieux**, author of
Dude, Where's My Jesus Fish?

All Peace
No Pieces

All Peace No Pieces

A COURSE IN MIRACLES' TAKE ON "THE WORLD"

Jackie Lora Jones

Foreword by Gary R. Renard

The Wisdom Series™ Book One

Jackie Lora Jones

PO Box 3501

Beverly Hills, CA 90212

jackie.news

Book Layout ©2017 BookDesignTemplates.com

All Peace No Pieces/ Jackie Lora Jones. — 1st Ed.

Library of Congress Control Number: 2018912424

ISBN 13: 978-0-578-40296-3 (Paperback edition)

ISBN 13: 978-0-578-40421-9 (eBook edition)

Contents

To my husband, Mark, I met you on my birthday and I can't think of a better gift. Thank you for everything. All my love.

Wisdom is not judgment;
it is the relinquishment of judgment.

–A COURSE IN MIRACLES

Acknowledgements

MY HEARTFELT GRATITUDE to my mother, Doris Lora, and my father, Ron Lora, for their unwavering love and unending support in my endeavors. Mom, thank you for contributing your insightful editing skills to this book. Dad, thank you for keeping me encouraged as I was writing it. I am grateful beyond measure for guidance you've both given me and for the example you've set.

I am beyond grateful to my wonderful sister, Cindy Lora-Renard, who is my sister forever in Spirit. I walk this path with you and I am filled with your inspiration, friendship and love every day.

To my step-mother, Alice Chumbley Lora, thank you for on-going reminders to treat myself with as much care as I treat others. I am grateful for the love of my late step-brother, Jeff Ray, and my step-sister, Leah Ray.

To all my family and friends, thank you for your love, insights and encouragement over the years. I am a lucky girl.

To the late Dr. Kenneth Wapnick, his wife Gloria Wapnick, and the Foundation for *A Course in Miracles*, your prolific teachings speak for themselves. I am deeply grateful to be able to continuously learn from you.

To Judy Skutch Whitson and The Foundation for Inner Peace, I am full of gratitude for the publication of this spiritual masterpiece. Thank you for following inspired guidance and bringing *A Course in Miracles* to millions around the world. I would like to acknowledge Judy's late husband, William "Whit" Whitson for his enormous contributions and efforts to spread the Course's message.

I would like to acknowledge and thank my husband, Mark Jones, for his care with this book. He made my "vision" for Book One come to life with his cover design and his attention to detail while formatting it.

Foreword
by Gary R. Renard

HAVING STUDIED SPIRITUALITY for 40 years, written four books, and traveled all over America and the rest of the world for the last 15 years teaching advanced spiritual principles, I can safely say there are precious few people who appear to be in this world who teach the modern spiritual masterpiece, *A Course in Miracles,* (ACIM), without compromising on its purely non-dualistic metaphysics, and who also stick to its emphasis on a certain kind of forgiveness. Jackie Lora Jones is one of those people. The fact that she happens to be my sister-in-law has no bearing on why I say that. Like her sister, my wife Cindy Lora-Renard, Jackie refuses to back down from the relentless truth that the Course offers the world. Indeed, if she or Cindy did, I wouldn't be able to work with them or write the forewords for their books.

Jackie also understands how and why the Course trains the mind to think along the lines of Spirit, which is perfect Oneness, rather than the separation of the ego. In order to learn it the student must make a conscious choice between one of two things, and only one of them is real. You have the truth of perfect Oneness, or God, which is reality, and then you have everything else, which is illusion. You must choose one or the other, and whichever one you choose will become what you believe is real, and will affect your experience.

It's not enough to go around saying, "The world is an illusion, the world is an illusion." That will leave you feeling empty and meaningless. You've got to *replace* the illusion with something else. This is where *A Course in Miracles* is much more proactive than people realize. The "Voice" of the Course doesn't stop at just doing an amazing job of exposing the nature of the ego and its belief in separation, which is where the dream of a universe of time and space came from. He, Jesus, whom I often call "J," completely replaces the thought system of the ego with the thought system of the Holy Spirit. As the Course says of the Holy Spirit, "He would not leave you alone in dreams of hell." Instead of leaving you dangling, the Holy Spirit teaches that the world of illusion can be replaced with the reality of Heaven. The world is imperfect and unstable in its functioning, but Heaven is perfect, which gives us a perfect home to go home *to.* And it's possible to experience the reality of this even while you appear to be here. That, of course, is a very advanced state, and once it's achieved then you are near the end of your illusory journey.

The primary tool for achieving the goal of the Course, enlightenment, is a completely uncompromising way of forgiveness, in which you overlook the body and engage in what the Course calls Vision. You think outside of the box; you think like the Holy Spirit does. It's not that you won't seem to see bodies with your body's eyes, but you look past them in your mind to the reality that is just beyond the veil. You forgive the images you see not from a position of being at the effect of them, but from a place of being at cause. The world eventually becomes like a puff of smoke you could blow away and see just beyond it to the truth that it was hiding from you.

This is impossible as long as you make the error real; as long as you give it your faith. We need to take that faith back and put it where it belongs: with God and His Kingdom. As the Course says, "Be vigilant only for God and His Kingdom." Grant you that's a tall order. But even though it's difficult, it *is* doable. The Holy Spirit wouldn't give us a job to do that couldn't be done.

Whether it's with this wonderful book, *All Peace No Pieces,* her excellent online video show, *The 24th Hour™,* her *True Forgiveness Teachings™* podcast, study group, or public speaking, Jackie demonstrates that she is a loving example of living the principles of ACIM. She also knows the difference between the self-help movement and real spirituality. The self-help movement is about getting what you want. Real spirituality is about being happy, strong and peaceful *regard-*

less of whether you get what you want, and being fearless no matter what appears to happen to you in the world. Ironically, you can do the Course and still have success. But I'll let Jackie explain that to you.

I can say with great confidence that *All Peace No Pieces* will help you, and accelerate you on your spiritual path. I thank Jackie for writing it. I'm also deeply grateful for my close friendship with Jackie and her husband Mark, who is a sound healer, among his other gifts, and a fascinating person. When the two of them and Cindy and I get together, the conversation is literally out of this world. The truth comes to us from outside of the system, as does this book. But be careful what you ask for. You may never look at the world the same way again.

— **Gary R. Renard**,
bestselling author of *The Disappearance of the Universe*

Prologue

I WALKED INTO THE BEDROOM of my Chicago condo in 1996. I looked around the room. I didn't know how I got there or what I was doing with my life. I burst into tears and fell forward on the bed exhausted. "Please help me," I said. Just then something came over me. I sat up and the tears stopped. All my worry seemed to subside. I had an overwhelming experience of peace. I couldn't believe the change from just a moment before — I knew what I had to do. The same voice I had heard all my life was once again giving me the gentle message to listen to my Higher Self and that "*everything will be okay.*"

I could either trust this inner guidance I'd heard all my life, or continue to live a life where I simply did what I thought others expected me to do.

I was never the same after that experience. I left my first marriage and moved back to California, where I had wanted to be since a very young age. Something was happening to me. I had so many questions about the direction of my life and no satisfying answers. I couldn't put my finger on it, but I knew that something was just not right with the world. I was waking up and about to experience a profound transformation.

Following that experience in Chicago I spent a few years in the "spiritual buffet line," trying all the different self-help techniques and manifesting exercises to make my life the way I wanted it to be. Then *A Course in Miracles* found me. It answered every question I've ever had. Peace had come and I had my purpose in life — awakening to Spirit.

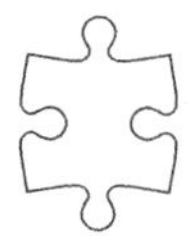

Introduction

I LOVE WATCHING *The Wizard of Oz* every year — I seldom miss it. The heroine of the story, Dorothy, falls asleep and dreams she is in a faraway land called Oz. She really believes she's there because it has become her reality for the moment. All Dorothy wants to do is go back home. She embarks on a journey to find the great and powerful Oz who she's told can help her get home.

On her wild journey following the yellow brick road, she meets companions along the way who each feel they lack something. The scarecrow wants a brain, the tin man wants a heart and the lion wants courage. The three of them join Dorothy and her dog Toto in search of what each one *believes* they need to be happy, and where they need to go to find it.

Along the way, the Wicked Witch of the West attempts to sabotage their journey, but Glinda, the Good Witch of the North, appears and helps them continue along their path.

Near the end of the story, Dorothy feels hopeless. The great and powerful Oz was not the answer after all. She still hasn't found her way home. With a gentle smile Glinda tells her that she's had the power within to go home all along. The scarecrow says, "Then why didn't you tell her before?" Glinda replies, "Because she wouldn't have *believed* me. She had to learn it for herself." As this thought sinks into Dorothy's mind her experience changes. She starts to believe it. She clicks her heels together and wakes up from her dream to find she never left the bed. She was home all along. It was just out of her awareness. All the craziness and insanity didn't *really* happen; it was just a dream. There was no Oz. She only believed there was. The Land of Oz was in her dreaming mind.

A Course in Miracles uses the metaphor of sleep to explain *our* life here in the world. It teaches that we *seemed* to fall asleep and are dreaming a dream of separation from our Creator — from our true state of perfect Oneness in Heaven. The Course reminds us that:

> **You are at home in God, dreaming of exile but perfectly capable of awakening to reality.[1]**

Like Dorothy, we don't know we're dreaming. We believe we're the figure in the dream instead of the dreamer of the dream. This world is not our home, but we *believe* it is because we've chosen a separation idea about ourselves in place of our true identity of oneness and unity. Our real life in Heaven has continued uninterrupted despite our attempts to dissociate it. It's outside of our awareness temporarily. The dream has become our reality. *A Course in Miracles* (ACIM or the Course) calls the whole universe time-space dream "the world." I wrote this book because I think more people are ready to end their suffering, get their questions answered, and wake up — as I was.

As a hypnotherapist and spiritual counselor for over a decade, I've heard the same questions and concerns from many, many people. Some of these same questions I asked myself while searching for answers in the "spiritual buffet line" in the 90's.

Why are things so chaotic in the world? Why is there continual strife and endless suffering? Why are things unfair? Why can't I make money doing something I enjoy? Why are relationships so hard? Do we have to struggle all the time? Why do bad things happen to good people? Don't I deserve to be happy? I wanted to understand why the world is the way it is.

I used to think the answers to the above questions would be found in information, people and circumstances "external" to myself. The right job or career, the right relationship, financial stability, having a supportive family and great friends, having a sense of purpose in the world, and so on. Dorothy's "futile" journey to the great and powerful Oz is symbolic of our always searching for answers from someone or something outside ourselves.

After several years of enjoying the self-help movement and its many beneficial teachings, I was still left unsatisfied. What was I looking for? Why were people always searching for something? I'll reveal in this book series why these limited approaches can get you only so far.

Fortunately, when I was discouraged I often indulged another part of myself growing up; I could hear a gentle voice in my head reminding me that "everything will be okay." I believed that voice and it gave me hope in some of my saddest and most depressing times. I would suddenly break out into a smile and feel good again. I was able to change my thoughts and feel better. That made me curious. I started paying attention to my thoughts. Little did I know that paying attention to my thoughts would end up being very important in the daily practice of *A Course in Miracles.*

ACIM teaches that the answer to inner peace, happiness and a sense of purpose is not found outside yourself. It comes about by how you're *thinking* about your life, not *what* happens in your life. What happens in your life will always feel like a roller coaster ride, full of shifts and changes, ups and downs. Can we ever depend on such instability to give us peace and joy?

In my own life things were often going my way one minute and then they would derail in the next. Why wasn't there consistency in my relationships? I wouldn't even know why or how things would derail —

they just would! What did I do? Just expressing a difference of opinion or sharing an experience I had would result in a massive argument. "This is insane," I thought.

ACIM is unique in that its focus isn't on fixing up the world. Its focus is on waking you up from your dream that there ***is*** a world. It helps us change our *mind* about the world. How does this help us with our relationships? It's amazing how this spiritual masterpiece helps heal all our relationships. I'll address what the Course calls "special relationships" throughout this book series and how to stay centered and come from a place of peace even in the most difficult of circumstances. Shifting and changing your behavior won't ultimately work. I'll show you how I changed my *mind* about my relationships.

ACIM teaches that the answers we're really looking for are not in the world. The main message of the Course is that:

> **There is no world. This is the central idea the Course attempts to teach.**[2]

However, there is a *belief* in the world. We are having an experience of being in the world as a body — it is a false experience — one we will eventually wake up from.

This advanced spiritual thought system answered every question I've ever had. I'll never forget reading *The Disappearance of the Universe* (Hay House, 2002), or "DU," by Gary Renard in 2004. I didn't know my now brother-in-law at the time. Although I had been enjoying the Course's teachings for several years, his book provided the last clarification I needed to not only understand its purely non-dualistic metaphysical message, but also led me to Ken Wapnick's prolific teachings on the Course and solidified that this was the path for me. This book naturally reflects the understanding gained from both of these authors.

I had been questioning the nature of the world all my life. Here was the last piece of the puzzle! However, my newfound way to *practice* the Course's principles was just beginning.

Throughout my adult life I've put to use my two areas of study: broadcast journalism and psychology. I enjoy helping people all over the world find inner peace through true forgiveness, no matter what is happening in their lives.

In Book One of "The Wisdom Series™," I'll discuss *A Course in Miracles*' take on "the world," how we *seemed* to get here, the importance of true forgiveness, what the miracle is, and the practical applications of the teachings I've applied in my own life. I will highlight Course themes I discuss on my podcasts, in workshops, with clients and in my Course group. My hope is that this book will lead you to a different *experience* of your life, specifically, to a more peaceful one regardless of what is happening to you and around you.

There will be much repetition as it is a necessary tool for unlearning what the ego has taught us. Those of you who know me know I love "reminders." That is one of the reasons I started my *True Forgiveness Teachings™* podcast. It offers reminders of the theory and practical application of *A Course in Miracles*.

How would you like to undo your *belief* in the false you so the real you is all that's left?

How different would your life be if you learned you have the answer within you to all your problems? What if all your many problems were seen as an opportunity to recognize what the Course calls our one and only problem?

I hope to convey in this series the benefits of how freeing it is to live with forgiveness instead of judgment, shared interests instead of separate interests, love instead of fear, and how to be in peace, not pieces.

A Course in Miracles is a path to permanent inner peace through forgiveness. It isn't a religion. It's a self-study curriculum that is practiced between you and the Holy Spirit or Jesus. The Holy Spirit and Jesus are the Course's *symbols* which I will use throughout this book to denote our inner teachers or Higher Self. I will also use italics throughout for emphasis.

Jesus redefines many terms in the Course from the way the world traditionally uses them: forgiveness, miracle, atonement, salvation, ego, and Holy Spirit to name a few. I will continue to redefine them as they come up throughout this book series to help clarify the Course's message.

The Course is not like anything else I've seen. It teaches that nothing outside yourself can have any effect on you unless given permission by you to do so.

I will share how ACIM taught me how to get what I *really* wanted — it's not what you think it is.

With that said, this poem entered my mind seemingly out of the blue a couple years ago when thinking about the purpose of this book:

Here is my purpose for writing this book
My hope is when anything disturbs you, you'll take a closer look

The ego will trick you and want to take charge
What is this "thing" that is speaking first and living large?

If something here in this world seems amiss
I can tell you from experience that something is this

We forgot we're dreaming, we think life in our body is real
Start thinking with the Holy Spirit, you have no idea how good you'll feel

Stay with me as the metaphysics are challenging to grasp
If you ever have a question, all you need do is ask

As you truly forgive it'll become quite clear
The less you'll be invested in what the ego holds dear

By choosing the miracle you'll start to awaken
This is the path you'll be glad you've taken

The Holy Spirit is speaking to the one mind that thinks it's here
As soon as you know this, the end of ego reign is probably near

Be of good cheer and whenever you want to scream
You can remember it's all a big dream!

Whenever you feel fearful, discouraged, sad, lonely, frightened, depressed or anxious, you can be sure something is amiss. You've identified with the false self; the ego. It's not you!

Welcome to a new way of thinking. Welcome to *A Course in Miracles*' take on "the world."

Be well & blessings,
Jackie Lora Jones

CHAPTER 1

How Did We Get Here?

...now our whole life, from birth unto death, with all its dreams, is it not in its turn also a dream, which we take as the real life, the reality of which we do not doubt only because we do not know of the other more real life? — Leo Tolstoy

When you have been caught in the world of perception you are caught in a dream. You cannot escape without help, because everything your senses show merely witnesses to the reality of the dream.[1]

I REMEMBER ONCE in the mid 2000's I saw a promo on ABC for an upcoming Barbara Walter's special on Heaven in which she asked, "Where is it?" and "How do we get there?"

I gazed at the TV answering her silently in my mind. "It's a state of perfect Oneness with our Creator, outside of time and space, and you're already there. You never left, you're just having a *dream* you left." I don't know how that answer would've been received had I been interviewed!

It is no coincidence that my two areas of interest in life were broadcast journalism and psychology. I always had questions running through my mind as to why things are the way they are in the world. Why did people behave in ways that hurt them? Why did I make decisions I would often regret because I wasn't being true to myself? My curiosity and awareness were heightened early in life when I became aware of my thoughts. I was watching myself think and I wondered if everyone did that. If you're someone who is aware of your thoughts, good for you. That's a good starting point.

I often noticed Jesus popping into my mind. However, my experience of Jesus was different than what traditional religion was presenting to me. For example, in regard to suffering, I thought, "Does it have to be this way?" The answer I heard in my mind was "no." Why? I wondered.

During my years in the spiritual buffet line, I first flirted with *A Course in Miracles* in 1999. It was teaching that there were two ways to look at things. The big blue book was a little intimidating when I'd see it every now and then in the bookstore, so I settled on a beautiful little book by Karen Casey called *Daily Meditations for Practicing the Course* (Hazelden, 1995). It was so helpful to me as a foray into a new way of looking at my life. The contrast between what the Course calls the ego's voice and the Holy Spirit's Voice became apparent. I was getting some answers and starting to put some pieces together.

I was still curious about the nature of the world. How could there be so much hatred, strife, sickness, depression, war, and toxicity? It was constant. Yes, we have good times mixed in and that's duality. You have the good and the bad, but the good never lasts. Something eventually happens, and we're sick again, depressed again, stressed again, or angry again. I wondered why certain people were able to catch breaks in life, while other really good-hearted people seemed to struggle. Why were we constantly comparing ourselves to others? All of us at one time or another ask questions such as "How could God have created this mess?" and "How do I make sure I get to Heaven?" Indeed, Barbara Walters traveled all over the world to find the answer.

I intuitively thought that God did not create this mess, but I didn't yet know why I thought that. I was still looking for answers. Albert Einstein famously said, "We can't solve problems using the same kind of thinking we used when we created them." Meanwhile, I continued reading Karen Casey's book, learning how to shift my thoughts and look at things differently whenever I felt anything but peaceful.

During this time period in the late 90's I moved from Los Angeles to Tennessee to co-host a morning show at a TV station outside of Memphis. A colleague said to me, "It's amazing that nothing seems to bother you. How do you do it?" I thought, "Something is working for me on a more permanent basis, because I am aware that I can change my mind whenever I choose to do so." I told her I'd been practicing the principles of a spiritual teaching called *A Course in Miracles* and that we have two parts to the mind. Our experience follows our thoughts and we can choose which voice we listen to throughout the day. Here is an excerpt from Karen's book I was reading at the time:

Joining with the Holy Spirit
Changes Everything

> There are many times throughout a day that we become consumed with resentment or fear or maybe even rage. Any of these feelings indicate we have been ensnared by the ego. It's also common to believe such feelings are justified. The ego claims to be right, always, regardless of the circumstances.
>
> Our obsession with our feelings is so overwhelming, we can't imagine letting them go...how wrong we are, but how gently the Course approaches us with an alternative path for living. It offers us the Holy Spirit as guide, comforter, friend, and controller. Joining with the Holy Spirit allows us to see every aspect of our lives differently and even makes letting go of all circumstances possible.[2]

How comforting is that! I felt so good about my new path! I had always been a positive person, but my awareness was expanding beyond just thinking positively. My intuitive abilities were also expanding.

Taking responsibility for my thoughts helped me adjust to the move to Tennessee, because it was daunting at first. I was used to living in Los Angeles and would now be living in a small town outside of Memphis. However, I was very excited to begin my first professional broadcasting job and knew it was the right move. Once again, my inner voice told me "Everything will be okay."

Not long after I adjusted to life in Tennessee, the television station changed its programming format and our morning show was no more. I was disappointed because I was having so much fun doing a job I was cut out for. However, after a short stint in New York and Chicago, I returned to Los Angeles knowing it was once again the right place to be.

It wasn't lost on me that after practicing the Course's principles for a while, my mind was already changing, favoring the importance of inner peace over anything else. This was an important moment for me. For example, I would've been much more disappointed about moving across the country and then the station changing format not too long after. I would have been somewhat anxious, thinking "What do I do now?" I imagine I would've felt forced to pursue another broadcasting job right away. However, my experience was just the opposite. I really went with "the flow." I knew that things were happening beyond my control and I could either put my salvation in my non-existent broadcasting career or experience inner peace, knowing that my self-worth was not wrapped up in a certain job, or proving anything to anyone. Wow! I felt peaceful even though I had an apartment full of furniture, a signed lease and no job! Why wasn't I more worried? I felt guilty for not feeling guilty!

One night after returning to Los Angeles my mother brought a book home from a Course group she was attending in the Pacific Palisades, an area in Los Angeles. She handed it to me and said, "Here are the answers you're looking for." Gary Renard's book, *The Disappearance of the Universe* or DU, as it's often referred to, changed everything! My mother and sister felt the same way. We had all been interested in *A Course in Miracles,* but did not grasp the depth of the purely non-dualistic message of this spiritual masterpiece until reading Gary's book, which continues to clarify the Course's teachings for so many. Little did we know at the time we were all reading DU that my sister would end up marrying Gary a few years later, and he would be part of our family. However, we did all have a sense (when reading DU) that we knew him somehow.

I think it was Gary's book that reminded me that the Course uses the metaphor of sleep to describe our state here in the world. The idea that we're dreaming caught my attention right away. I knew there was something going on here! I just couldn't quite put my finger on it.

Our life in the body is not our true reality. The Course tells us:

> **You recognize from your own experience that what you see in dreams you think is real while you are asleep. Yet the instant you waken you realize that everything that seemed to happen in the dream did not happen at all.[3]**

The Course further reminds us:

> **You dwell not here, but in eternity. You travel but in dreams, while safe at home.[4]**

I started doing the workbook of the Course after reading DU for the second or third time. I also started reading the text more closely — with great excitement and heightened understanding.

As I mentioned in the introduction, ACIM answered every question I've ever had. It helped me put the pieces of the puzzle together regarding my questions about the world. I was excited to continue practicing its principles with deeper awareness. We are not *really* suffering here. We're having a *dream* that we're suffering. I realized why my answer was "no" to the question I had asked so long ago; "Does it have to be this way?" "This is very empowering," I thought.

One of the most eye-opening statements in the Course that helped me integrate and accelerate my daily practice is when Jesus (who is identified by its scribe Helen Schucman as the Voice of *A Course in Miracles* and speaks in the first person throughout) asks us:

What if you recognized this world is an hallucination? What if you really understood you made it up? What if you realized that those who seem to walk about in it, to sin and die, attack and murder and destroy themselves, are wholly unreal? Could you have faith in what you see, if you accepted this?[5]

And further:

Hallucinations disappear when they are recognized for what they are. This is the healing and the remedy.[6]

I resonated with this immediately. So why would we dream up a world in the first place? Let's start with a brief story of how we *seemed* to get here in the world.

The Ego's Myth of Separation: The Journey into Sin, Guilt & Fear

God is not the author of fear. You are.[7]

In the beginning there was only perfect Oneness. *A Course in Miracles* teaches that:

Into eternity, where all is one, there crept a tiny, mad idea, at which the Son of God remembered not to laugh.[8]

This "tiny mad idea" was the idea that we could somehow be separate from our Creator, from our perfect Oneness in Heaven. What *seemed* to occur was a collective thought of, "What if I went off on my own to play outside of Heaven and perfect Oneness?" "What if I separated from All that is?" The Course uses the word "seemed" because the Atonement principle, according to the Course, says we've never separated from Heaven because it's impossible to be anything other than what God created us to be, whole and innocent.

> **Heaven is here. There is nowhere else. Heaven is now. There is no other time.**[9]

When I realized that this is a purely non-dualistic thought system which means it recognizes God as the *only* reality — everything else is an illusion of our making — I believed it. I thought, "Okay, what do I do with that?" And "How do I get back to that awareness?" And further, "What do I do when I'm here living my life while I know this?" The Course teaches that true forgiveness is the way back, which we'll get into. It's a wonderful practice! However, how Jesus explains forgiveness in ACIM is different than the traditional form of forgiveness that we've been taught, maybe that we've grown up with. The Course teaches us how to integrate the idea that God is the only reality with living here now, and with this new awareness. Living in a gentler dream with this new awareness precedes awakening to our true state of perfect oneness in Heaven.

Three Parts to the Mind and the Importance of Choice

As mentioned earlier, the Course uses the metaphor of sleep to describe the false idea of separation. Continuing our story above, once we *seemed* to fall asleep as God's collective one son, there are now two interpretations of this "tiny mad idea" that we could be separate from our Source.

The part of our mind the Course calls the Holy Spirit represents the right mind. This part of us knows it's impossible to be separate from perfect Love. The Holy Spirit is the memory of our true home that we took with us into the dream when we fell asleep. The *belief* in separation was corrected in the same instant it seemed to occur, which is the atonement principle. Atonement in ACIM corrects our belief in the separation, saying *nothing has happened*.

There's another part of the mind the Course calls the ego or wrong mind. The ego's interpretation is that the separation actually happened and is true. This is the beginning of the "special" or separate self. This part of the mind loves being in charge and being the boss. What goes hand-in-hand with separation is the accompanying belief in sin, guilt, fear, scarcity, lack and so forth.

Growing up, I always felt that there was someone or something else in my mind giving me messages when I was depressed or sad. The thought was, "Everything will be okay." I realize now that I was vacillating between these two thought systems, the ego and the Holy Spirit. This explains why I would suddenly be able to let things go, or be able to feel better even if my circumstances or surroundings didn't change.

The third part of the mind is the decision-maker (a term the Course does not use in this context but always implies), which we'll also call the "observer." Ken

Wapnick, in his prolific teachings, refers to the part of the mind that chooses between the ego and the Holy Spirit as the decision-maker, because Jesus reminds us throughout the Course that we have the power of choice; indeed, the Course says the choice of either the ego or Holy Spirit is our one remaining power in the dream. We can choose to see it with true perception. Jesus continually reminds us to "choose once again," whenever we are anything less than peaceful. He asks us to do this when we're not peaceful because that's when we're motivated to make a change! The change he suggests we make is never external; it's changing our internal teacher.

The Decision for the Ego Is Our Only Problem

What happened next is that we, now aware of two ways to interpret the idea of separation as the decision-making part of the mind, chose to listen to the ego instead of the Holy Spirit. We couldn't help but want to be a special, autonomous self. We're still making that choice right now!

The ego further tells us that in order for the separation to have happened, we had to disconnect from God through attack and kill him off. This was our "sin." *Sin* according to ACIM is synonymous with separation and lack of love. We then felt *guilty* that we chose to go out on our own, as if Heaven wasn't enough. We thought we could do better! Remember the prodigal son story?

The enormous *guilt* we felt for killing off God in favor of a better way brought on enormous *fear*! The ego, which is still only a silly false idea the mind has made up, has now convinced us that God will punish us for separating from the whole. We, in our collective separated state, have now made up a punishing God instead of remembering the true loving God. As Voltaire said, "If God created us in His image, we have certainly returned the compliment."

God created us as perfect Spirit, purely Love, but we rejected that idea in favor of being on our own and autonomous — the opposite of Spirit. Because we *believe* we're now separate from the whole, and that we've sinned, we believe God is angry and will punish us. We play out this fear of God idea in our everyday lives.

The Introduction of Projection

This terror makes us want to run and hide to escape God's seeming wrath. Of course this is the ego's made-up God. Our Father in Heaven has never acknowledged the separation and therefore would not respond to it. That would make it *real.* This is why we have a completely safe home of perfect love to return to. Workbook Lesson 160 states:

> **I am at home. Fear is the stranger here.**[10]

As we follow the ego's separation myth further, our guilt is so intense that we leave the realm of the mind through the psychological device of *projection* to escape God's punishment. This enormous projection of guilt outward can be thought of as what scientists refer to as the Big Bang. The Course notes that this massive projective explosion outward resulted in the whole made-up universe of time and space, that is, "the world."

Since the ego convinced us that we could get rid of our guilt through projection, but protect our specialness, we went for it! Now that we have taken on an individual existence as a body in "the world," we have forgotten we made this up. The body only exists to experience separation. It was a big part of the ego's plan to keep us mindless, lost in a world of dreams. Our choice for separation is now unconscious to us. We are lost in a dream we *believe* is really happening. We seemingly took our *thought* of separation in the mind as one collective son and fragmented it into billions and billions of pieces. These are the "effects." These effects include the individual bodies we *believe* ourselves and others to be. These pieces are also atoms, cells, bacteria, animals, rocks, trees, star systems, galaxies — anything and everything that has a form. All forms in this projection we call "the world" are symbolic of the one mistaken *thought* of separation.

> **Consider all the distortions you've made of nothing; all the strange forms and feelings and actions and reactions that you have woven out of it.**[11]

Much Ado about Nothing!

We made-up this whole universe of time and space out of nothing! Why is it nothing? Because the separation did not occur. This is the atonement principle. Atonement has a different meaning in the Course than what Christianity teaches. Christianity teaches that we, as bodies, have to "atone" for our sins, making the idea of sin real, and consequently, the whole world real. Atonement in the Course is "the correction of our belief in sin", affirming that the separation has not occurred.

There is a Way Out: Forgiveness and the Miracle

What do we do here knowing the world is an illusion of our own making? Thank goodness we have Jesus, the Holy Spirit, forgiveness and the miracle! This is the way back home. We still live our normal lives here; however, we live under a different set of principles or mindset. This is how we begin the process toward enlightenment. Enlightenment in the Course is awakening from the dream of separation and duality.

When I practice true forgiveness, I'm reminded of the section in the Course called "The Hero of the dream." The body is the ego's crowning glory! Everything we see, hear, smell, taste and touch witnesses to the reality of the dream — the reality of the separation — that's what the body was *made* to do! What I've found in my life as I've practiced giving my day over to Jesus or the Holy Spirit, is that my mind retranslates everything I see. Every time I'm upset, sad, anxious, annoyed and so forth, everything is now used as a classroom to get me home, meaning my *purpose* for "the world" has changed. It's not about denying the world, but rather denying the ego's interpretation of what I'm seeing in favor of the Holy Spirit's interpretation. This makes all the difference. This is how we start. How do we do it? Well, we have every opportunity — all around us, all the time.

We start our practice of forgiveness out in the illusory world, not because it's really there, but because we *believe* it is and that's what our current experience is. So we start by forgiving all the symbols; all the pieces — ourselves, other people, and circumstances that we see and experience in the world. We pay attention to upsets and grievances and look at them through right-minded perception. We forgive them for what they haven't really done. Why? Because we remember that it's our projection and things in a projection aren't real. That's why no one has really done anything. The world is coming *from* us as a dreaming mind. It's not being done *to* us. So anytime we get upset, anytime we are anything less than peaceful — that is our opportunity. That's the red flag reminder to say, "Here's the way back. Here's my chance." Instead of furthering illusions, I can wake up from them by practicing true forgiveness.

As I go through my day, I know I'm going to have an opportunity in which I'm not peaceful. Something inevitably happens. No matter how big or small it is, that's the opportunity to notice my thoughts and notice my upset feelings. I go back to the mind and remember I'm the dreamer of this dream and I can forgive my projected images and myself for projecting them. Then I let go. The Holy Spirit's thought system *replaces* the ego's thought system. This is my new starting point. I move forward with this new awareness. I'm living normally here, but I'm now interpreting everything differently — through the lens that brings peace to the mind and helps me wake up.

The miracle, in *A Course in Miracles*, shows us who the dreamer is. It brings us back to the mind, so we can view our lives through the Holy Spirit's lens instead of the ego's. We shift our perception from the ego's way of looking at the illusory world, to the Holy Spirit's. Practicing forgiveness has been so beneficial for me. What I've noticed is that "Jackie", the personal self, was transformed first. As the Holy Spirit starts to take over your mind, you're gentler, kinder, and looking at everyone the same, meaning, we're all in fear because we believe we're here. This is the sameness we share - we all believe we're separate, but also share the Holy Spirit in our minds.

Why Does the Course Say There Is No World?

One of the Course's main tenets is:

> **Ideas leave not their source.**[12]

This means the idea of separation has never left its *source* in the dreaming mind. Hence, there is no world out there, projected or otherwise. The world is still in the mind. This helps us understand the famous quote most students know from the Course:

> **Seek not to change the world, but choose to change your mind about the world.**[13]

Why should we seek to change our mind? Because mind is the *cause*, the world is the *effect*. If you want change, you have to go to the source of all conflict.

The source of all our pain and suffering, both physiological and psychological, is symbolic of first choosing the idea of separation in the mind. Without separation there is no world and no bodies to inhabit it. The choice for separation (the ego tells us) is an attack on God. This produced a guilt so horrible that we had to *deny* we were responsible and thus project the thought outside the mind. Notice how the decision for guilt plays out in our lives here: we feel guilty and punish either ourselves or others every day in many different ways, in both thought and word. Psychology 101 tells us two things: One, that guilt demands punishment, and two, projection follows denial. We have denied the truth of who we are in favor of an autonomous self.

> **Of one thing you were sure: Of all the many causes you perceived as bringing pain and suffering to you, your guilt was not among them.**[14]

The ego thought system's *content* is guilt. Projecting our guilt outward does not get rid of it since "ideas leave not their source." The guilt is still in the mind and needs to be forgiven. The ego has temporarily succeeded in keeping us away from the mind through the mechanism of projection, however, we also are free to choose the Holy Spirit or Jesus at any time and start to wake up from this dream of duality.

To summarize, projection outward does not get rid of our unconscious guilt since "ideas leave not their source." The guilt is still in the mind and needs to be forgiven. Furthermore, the Holy Spirit heals us on all levels. When we do our part, He takes care of the part of the mind that's unconscious to us.

Once we make the choice for the Holy Spirit or Jesus we start to undo the *belief* in the false self. We recall the projection. We start to heal this unconscious guilt one forgiveness lesson at a time. We start to wake up from our belief in sin. This is how we move from nightmare dreams to happy dreams. The happy dreams of forgiveness are still part of the illusion, but they wake us up instead of furthering illusion. We move from being fearful to being peaceful. Jesus helps us do this slowly.

> **So fearful is the dream, so seeming real, he could not waken to reality without the sweat of terror and a scream of mortal fear, unless a gentler dream preceded his awakening, and allowed his calmer mind to welcome, not to fear, the Voice that calls with love to waken him; a gentler dream, in which his suffering was healed and where his brother was his friend.**[15]

Our learning has gotten us to wherever we are. Now we have a choice to make if we're tired of suffering. *Which teacher do we follow in the dream?* One keeps us dreaming and the other wakes us up. True forgiveness is what wakes us up. Not being taken in by appearances wakes us up. I know you've probably heard the saying, "we're all in this together." We truly are. When we make either choice, for the ego or the Holy Spirit, we make the choice for the *entire Sonship* because all minds are joined being that there's only one. We are either teaching love or teaching fear in each moment, depending on which interpretation of the dream we choose to listen to. Through consistent choice for the Holy Spirit's forgiveness classroom, we eventually find ourselves back in the home we never truly left. Let's wake up to the awareness that we are all peace. No pieces.

CHAPTER 2

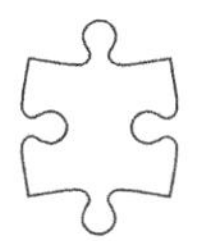

Why Is the World Insane?

The world is false perception. It was born of error and it has not left its source. It will remain no longer than the thought that gave it birth is cherished. When the thought of separation has been changed to one of true forgiveness, will the world be seen in quite another light; and one which leads to truth, where all the world must disappear and all its errors vanish.[1]

According to "the world" we have to atone for our sins or we will be punished. We aren't worthy of Heaven without sacrifice. This is insane! The Course uses the term "insane" or "insanity" in the accurate, currently legal sense — meaning "out of touch with reality." When we believe we are separate from our Source, we are insane and indeed out of touch with our true reality of being at home with God.

In addition, we still often believe the ego lie that we have sinned and need to earn God's love. For Dorothy, in order to be "worthy" of help from the Wizard, she is asked to go through extreme hardship. She must bring him the broomstick of the Wicked Witch of the West. Her wish to go home will only be granted with "conditions" attached. How horrible is this task! The Wizard's request induces enormous fear. His cruel demands can only be what masquerades as power. This insanity can only be of the ego. There is no power in sacrifice, yet this is what the ego would teach us.

This world is insane and cannot be our real home, because everything here involves sacrifice. The underlying premise is that we are not worthy. We unconsciously believe we've sinned against God for choosing separation from Him. Our guilt over this demands punishment and sacrifice. We go through life having to prove ourselves in one way or another. Not only that, but we are all born lacking something someone else seems to have. If we only had this or that, then things would be different, we say.

> **A sense of separation from God is the only lack you really need correct. This sense of separation would never have arisen if you had not distorted your perception of truth, and had thus perceived yourself as lacking.**[2]

The ego thought system is based not only on guilt, but on lack. The scarecrow thinks he needs a brain, the tin man thinks he needs a heart, and the lion thinks he lacks courage. We are taught we have to earn everything here, or that it has to be bestowed upon us by someone worthier or better than we are. We suffer and sacrifice ourselves in order to be worthy of God's love. Does this feel right to you?

Dorothy puts her faith in the Wizard to get home. She's looking outside herself for her salvation. As we know, it didn't work. He couldn't get her home. The Wizard represents the ego's false game of hope, enticing us to put our faith in a myriad of distractions other than God. It is the carrot and stick metaphor. Dorothy and her companions make a false idol out of the Wizard and end up disappointed. With blunt clarity, the Course says the ego's motto is "seek and do not find."

Other examples of false idols are what the Course calls our "special love" and "special hate" relationships. Jesus teaches that our idols of special love and special hate are both meaningless. They never bring us what we *really* want. When our idols of special love (which can take the form of significant others or spouses) disappoint us because our needs aren't met, they quickly become the idols of special hate. So, idols we worship in our dream can be people, objects or problems. And who would we be without our problems? An idol, then, is a symbolic term for the substitution of the ego in place of our true Self or God. This *belief* in the ego thought system is projected out onto these special love and special hate relationships in the world. "Special" means "separate" from our one true relationship with God in Heaven.

The problem of addictions, for example, can be seen as making a false idol out of things outside ourselves: people, substances, sex, gambling, shopping and food, to name a few. What we're really addicted to is the ego thought system, which says we have sinned and therefore will be punished. We're unconsciously attracted to sin because the ego tells us it proves we've usurped God's power and become our own "special" autonomous self. This faulty thought can play out in the *form* of a physical or psychological addiction to something or someone in the world.

To the ego, the form an idol takes in the world makes no difference as long as we believe our salvation can be found there, keeping us looking for answers outside of ourselves instead of going within. Going within in the Course means going back to the mind. Our focus on the myriad of idols in the world serves the ego's goal of keeping us mindless - away from the mind's power to choose against its false perception in favor of the Holy Spirit's truth. The Course states plainly:

> **It is vain to worship idols in the hope of peace. God dwells within, and your completion lies in Him. No idol takes His place. Look not to idols. Do not seek outside yourself.**[3]

As soon as one idol falls, the ego has another ready to go! This time we'll get the right job or have a better relationship. This diet will be the one. That doctor will find out what's wrong with me. This time I won't buy so much, or drink or eat so much, we say. As soon as we believe one problem is solved, another one appears that needs our immediate attention. Sometimes our guilt takes the same form over and over. This is the nature of the ego's world, folks! The carrot and the stick metaphor. It's insanity and cannot be real.

In ACIM, Jesus gently corrects our *belief* in sin, saying that the separation from our Creator was a mistaken choice made by a dreaming mind. This dreaming mind wanted to play on its own outside of Perfect Oneness and Unity. But — mistakes call for correction, not punishment. Jesus reminds us we are free to "choose once again." We can choose the atonement for ourselves. Atonement in the Course is the correction of our *belief* in sin. Accepting the atonement principle is our salvation.

> Salvation is the Atonement, or undoing of the separation; we are "saved" from our *belief* in the reality of sin and guilt through the change of mind that forgiveness and the miracle bring about.[4]

The world is insane because it's based on the insane *thought* that we have sinned and that we *are* sin. We feel guilty for this perceived sin and fear we're going to be punished. Again, Psychology 101 tells us guilt demands punishment. The ego has tricked us into thinking we killed off God in order to usurp his power and be our own boss. When we realized we threw away Heaven in favor of a unique special self, this produced unconscious guilt so terrible that we feared immense punishment. The ego tells us this myth is true and by our choice we "believed" it. We took the "tiny mad idea" seriously which means it produced effects. What are the effects? The whole universe of time and space.

We listen to the ego thought system over and over again in its myriad forms, thinking eventually it will offer us our salvation. Before finding ACIM I always felt like a hamster on a wheel. I'll get into how I practically apply these teachings and the importance of staying vigilant!

Your salvation is not anywhere in the world. How can there be sanity in a world that's based on the idea of sin, guilt and fear? Not only that — the unholy trinity of sin, guilt and fear is a completely false idea! The Course mentions the word insane 195 times, the word insanely 10 times, and the word insanity 66 times! I think Jesus is trying to tell us something!

> **You cannot evaluate an insane belief system from within it. Its range precludes this. You can only go beyond it, look back from a point where sanity exists and *see the contrast.* Only by this contrast can insanity be judged as insane.**[5]

So when Jesus says "you can only go beyond it and look back from a point where sanity exists," he's talking about going back to the decision maker in your mind: Your power of choice. This is the one remaining power you have in this world; you can choose to see it for what it is.

When we choose to return to our decision-making mind, we become a right-minded *observer*. We become the dreamer of the dream and recognize our *real* identity is not the figure in the dream (our individual selves). Our individual self is a false identity based on separation. There is no dream without the body. The ego made the body — the hero of the dream — which exists only to experience separation. This keeps us away from the mind. Remember, the ego thought system of sin, guilt and fear is responsible for the projection of the whole physical universe of time and space, which includes all our bodies. When we become a right-minded observer, we look without judgment with Jesus or the Holy Spirit at the insanity of the ego thought system. It's important that when we get upset at ourselves or others, we use that "red flag" of being upset as an opportunity to change our internal teacher. This is how we practice *A Course in Miracles.* Can it be that simple — have the "little willingness" to look at things differently? Yes. Is it *easy* to do? No! Let's help each other!

While most people would agree that the world is insane, they're still asleep when it comes to *why* it's insane and unaware as to what's really going on. We hit a wall because, until we're aware, we only understand it's insane from *within* the system, within the falsity of the ego framework. We don't know how to escape it without help. We're trapped.

Fortunately, ACIM gives us a way back through the power of true forgiveness and the resulting miracle. It's not the only way, but it's a great way for those drawn to this spiritual thought system. Instead of furthering illusions, we can wake up from them. This is the function of true forgiveness and the miracle.

CHAPTER 3

True Forgiveness and the Miracle

> Forgiveness is not an occasional act; it is a constant attitude. — Martin Luther King, Jr.

WHEN I WAS in my teens, I had some very sad and confusing moments because there was a person — supposedly a friend — who was unkind to me for a long time. I was baffled by it because I'd never done anything to warrant the behavior, but since my self-esteem was not great at times, I was afraid to confront this person. I didn't even talk much about it with my close friends; I wish I had, because I learned later that a couple of them had a similar experience.

Years later I thought about the situation and forgave the person in my mind. My thought was, "This person was doing the best she could at the time and was insecure herself, just like I often was at that age." I understood why she acted badly towards me. Someone told me years later that she was actually jealous of me. "Why?" I thought. That would never have occurred to me. Anyway, I forgave her (so I thought), but there was still a hurtful "pang" in me when thinking about it. I felt like I was "over" it, but I still did not have an interest in seeing her again, because the memories of what happened — along with memories of untrue rumors I was told she spread about me — were still hurtful.

Several years after that, she popped into my mind again. By this time I had been practicing the Course for several years and had a very different experience of those memories that I'll share with you.

As we've already seen, Jesus redefines many terms in the Course from the way the world traditionally uses them: forgiveness and the miracle are two of these terms.

A Course in Miracles doesn't leave us hanging. There are other spiritual paths that also teach that this world is an illusion, mostly eastern traditions like Hinduism and Buddhism. But what do we do with that information? ACIM is unique because it is proactive in a way that uses our illusory experience as a tool here to get us back to our real home in Heaven. It does this by giving us the Holy Spirit's thought system to replace the ego's thought system. This is how we awaken from the dream; we can gently invite the Holy Spirit to undo what the ego has wrongly taught us — eliminating a feeling of hopelessness while we're living our normal lives here. When I learned the Course's definition of forgiveness and the miracle, and how to apply the teachings in my daily life, it changed my perception of everything! Notably, it changed my interpretation of all the painful memories that would pop up now and then throughout my adult life.

True forgiveness says that nothing outside ourselves can take the peace of God away. Why? Because we made up the world and can choose to withdraw our *belief* in and *attachment* to what we made.

Forgiveness is how we let go of all separation ideas and put the pieces back together! It is the key to happiness, but you have to turn the key! How can you unlock a door without turning the key?

ACIM teaches that forgiveness is an "attitude," a state of mind. It is not an occasional act done simply when someone or something does you wrong, although it does start out that way for most of us. When we feel wronged or when we observe ourselves or someone else behaving badly, and it affects us, these are the red flags the Course says that alert us there's a problem, because we're not at peace. We start there. ACIM teaches that we can go through our lives with a forgiving attitude; we can be "miracle-ready" instead of "judgment ready". Forgiveness is the way back to sanity. When you don't truly forgive, you hold yourself and the other person or situation prisoner. True forgiveness in A *Course in Miracles* says we forgive our brothers for what they *haven't* really done because we made them up in the first place, so what we're seeing isn't true:

> **Forgiveness recognizes what you thought your brother did to you has not occurred. It does not pardon sins and make them real. It sees there was no sin. And in that view are all your sins forgiven.[1]**

This seems strange at first, only because we forgot that what we're forgiving are merely fragments of a projection that is coming from our own mind. Not our brain, which is part of the hardware of the body, but coming from the one collective mind outside time and space that thinks it is separate from God. So we are forgiving the contents of our collective split mind. These fragments or "pieces" have taken many forms. Our body and other bodies being some of the forms.

This is difficult to comprehend, especially when we turn on the news and hear horrific stories of child abuse and animal cruelty. It feels impossible to think of forgiving the perpetrators. How could they commit these acts? I know in my own life I've had some major forgiveness opportunities around abuse of both people and animals. My clients have shared their struggles with serious illnesses and ask, "How can I forgive this?"

We all have probably wondered at times, "Does it mean someone is off the hook when I forgive them? Shouldn't they be held accountable for their actions? I can forgive them because everyone makes mistakes, but will they ever learn?" Or when bad things happen to us, we ask, "How could this have happened to me?" Logically, this is how we think when we're in the ego mind. When we listen to the ego, we ask these questions from the *belief* that what people have done is real, or we believe what is happening to our own body is real, because we believe we *are* the body. It's our identity. We think the world and all that happens in it is our real life, and understandably so. After all, it's all we know.

ACIM leads us beyond body-limited experience when we're ready. Can we truly forgive people when we believe they've really done something? Can we truly forgive God when we get sick if we believe he created us *as bodies*? The Course says no. Why did the experience in my childhood of being treated unkindly still make me sad years later? The Course would say "because you still believe it's true, or else you wouldn't feel bad." Let's look at why the world's form of forgiveness, although helpful at times, never brings us what we really want — true, consistent inner peace and happiness.

The world's idea of forgiveness is very different from what ACIM teaches. The world's form of forgiveness is forgiving people because they've really done something. Indeed in the dream they have. We often forgive people for one of these reasons: We've gotten over what they did or moved past it. We're "the bigger person", more advanced or spiritual, older and wiser now, or we identify with the familiar quote from the Bible, "Father forgive them for they know not what they do."

All the above examples of the world's form of forgiveness spring from the ego's false premise: the world outside of us is real. We are a body separate from everyone else and are at the mercy of our circumstances here.

A few more examples are helpful here in grasping the Course's radical meaning of forgiveness. If something or someone upsets us, but we choose to let it go instead of holding onto it, this is a noble idea and a good start. But let's think of where our minds are when we think this way. Being able to let something go because we want to feel peace still makes the illusion real, because there's still the *you* that's letting go because the person really did something. Who is the "you" that's letting go? This "you" is the self that believes you're a body. That belief allows what is outside of you to affect you because you've forgotten that what you're "seeing" is your own projection. How can an illusion affect you? Only if the mind *believes* in it, can it affect you. Believing in the "you" and forgiving from one body to another is a separation idea that *keeps the ego thought system real to your mind, even if it doesn't "bother" you anymore.* This is key.

Secondly, there are those of us who forgive because we're on a spiritual path. Our inner work over the years helps us look at things differently and we learn that forgiveness is really for "us." We're then able to let go of our anger or hurt so we're not paralyzed and we can move on in a healthy way with our life. Sound familiar? Again, a noble effort, and congratulations on recognizing that forgiveness benefits you as well as the person you're forgiving. However, it still reinforces to your mind that you're really here on a spiritual path and that it's important that "you" (as a body) move on with your life. The Course would say "what life?" This is not your real life here.

> **There is no life outside of Heaven. Where God created life, there life must be. In any state apart from Heaven life is illusion.[2]**

The Holy Spirit wants to keep us focused on undoing the idea that we're separate bodies, not reinforce it.

Third, if we have compassion for others and resonate with the famous Bible quote, "Father forgive them, for they know not what they do," this is still a separation idea. We have compassion for them because we rationalize that they were probably doing the best they could, given their awareness at that moment. Don't get me wrong; this is a kinder, gentler attitude, and can indeed be a helpful step in the right direction as are the other examples above, but what are we really doing? Again, we are judging someone as different from us by believing that they're going through a rough time and so we can excuse their behavior. This is still a separation idea. There's you and them. That makes the whole ego thought system real to your mind, which does not undo your unconscious guilt.

This is where I was with my childhood friend. I forgave her because I realized she was in pain too, but I still judged her behavior as real in my mind and believed she really was unkind to me. Yes, there is no denying that these things do happen in the world, and she was unkind to me, as Jackie. But Jesus is reminding us to shift our focus from these illusory happenings in the world to us as bodies, and go back to the mind to address the cause. This approach is indeed a high bar.

> **Miracle-minded forgiveness is *only* correction. It has no element of judgment at all. The statement 'Father forgive them for they know not what they do' in no way evaluates *what* they do. It is an appeal to God to heal their minds. There is no reference to the outcome of the error. That does not matter.[3]**

The outcome of the error (belief in separation) Jesus is referring to is what happens in the world (the effects). What needs to be forgiven is the mind's *decision* for the ego. The mind's decision for the false self is what made up everything you experience in the world for the purpose of keeping you away from the solution — the mind's ability to choose the Holy Spirit. We only need correction at the mind level; then the effects will take care of themselves.

Fourth, let's say something doesn't bother you anymore. When that person or situation pops into your mind, you might think something like, "I'm glad I got over that." That may feel good to not care anymore, but it's still real in your mind because there is an "I" that got over something someone else really did. *This makes the whole ego thought system real to you and will not undo the belief in separation required to wake you up from the dream.* Furthermore, when your unconscious guilt remains in place, you'll keep having new things come up that you have to forgive. Your unconscious guilt over the *seeming* separation from God can take the same form over and over, or take a different form. If you only forgive something on the surface because it no longer bothers you, something else will take its place because the *source* of the guilt in the mind has not been looked at. You'll just project your unconscious guilt onto something or someone else. This is key to remember in your daily practice.

The Course would call all the above reasons forgiveness-to-destroy (talk about setting a high bar). Meaning, we can't really forgive others when we're coming from the ego thought system of separation, because believing in separation won't heal our unconscious guilt. When we believe people are separate from us and judge those differences, we are joining with the ego in them. It reinforces that we're actually separate from one another and our Creator. We are truly kind and can truly forgive only when we're listening to the inner teacher of kindness — the Holy Spirit or Jesus. This is difficult to understand from the world's perspective because it seems like we're being kind and loving when we sympathize, empathize or have compassion for "other people." However, since we believe there are really "other people," we remain trapped in the ego thought system. Once again, Jesus would remind us that what we're seeing is an outside picture of the inner thought system of guilt we've made real in our mind. He wants to help us undo the *cause* in our mind, which is the decision for guilt over innocence.

Being compassionate, kind and thoughtful towards others is automatically *extended* through you when you're coming from your right mind. You won't even have to think about it. You won't have to try to be kind or thoughtful. You won't be concerned if someone is accepting your forgiveness. Your focus will be on undoing the idea in your mind that the person is separate from you. What you do or say after this recognition is just the effect, which you never have to worry about. The healing occurs in the mind and then the effect plays itself out *through* you.

All the above default reasons for forgiveness share the common premise that the world is reality, so naturally we think people have really done something to us. We don't need to feel bad about thinking this way. How would we know otherwise? Any forgiveness thoughts you have are helpful and a step in the right direction if you are becoming less judgmental and more loving. Let's remember that. However, Jesus does clarify ACIM's teaching on why its forgiveness process is different, and how it will bring us what we *truly* want deep down inside. It answered my questions as to why I could never really feel peaceful, even though throughout my life I typically "took the high road" and gave people the benefit of the doubt. I was able to let go of a lot of things. However, there was still "me" and "them" in my mind. This isn't true forgiveness as the Course teaches and will only keep your mind asleep and dreaming. If you believe any part of the illusion is true, to your mind *all* of it is true.

Remember that the ego is the false idea that we've separated from our Creator. The ego is a substitute self (body) for the real Self (perfect Spirit) God created. If the cause of the world is false, and never really happened, then the effect of that, the world and everything in it, must also be false.

The essence of forgiveness is seeing others' interests as the same as yours. Everyone here is in fear and wants to awaken from nightmares and remember their innocence. This is the template you hold in your awareness.

This can be daunting at first, but with commitment and practice, withdrawing our investment in illusions offers great relief. It is a relief because we start to understand that there's only one problem to which there is one solution. The problem is our *belief* in separation. The problem isn't the separation itself because it never really occurred. The solution is the atonement principle:

> **The Holy Spirit's plan of correction to undo the ego and heal the belief in separation.**[4]

With regard to my example of being treated unkindly by a friend in my teens, I thought of this again after several years of practicing the Course and here's what happened.

I had a nocturnal dream one night and this girl appeared in my dream and gave me a big hug! I woke up feeling that I had truly forgiven her on another level. I remembered that I had made her up and she was part of the mind's projection. I didn't make her up on this level, where I experienced being sad, but rather I had chosen this script on another level and it was just playing itself out. When the thought of her came up, I now had another way of looking at the situation. I looked at it with Jesus by my side reminding me that I could forgive it because nothing had really happened except in a dream. There was no separation between us, only a thought of separation. I literally felt so much peace, unlike anything I had ever felt before regarding this girl. Is the mind this powerful? Yes! I learned that we forgive not because we're good spiritual people, but because what we're seeing isn't true. Because I was "miracle-ready" when the thought of her came up (instead of "judgment-ready" and thinking of her as separate from me), my *experience* changed to one of peace. What a miracle!

Forgiveness is the home of miracles.[5]

The Miracle

It's so interesting how many times ACIM students hear the phrase, "The Course is simple, but not easy." It's simple because all we're asked to do is look at the ego without judgment — which means *looking* at our grievances and upsets with Jesus or the Holy Spirit. It is simple because the truth is simple. It's not easy because the ego is so complicated! It takes vigilant and dedicated practice to undo our belief in the ego. Part of the ego is our individual self. Without the ego there is no special individual self, and this is what frightens us.

A miracle according to ACIM is not anything physical having to do with external phenomena happening in the world.

> **A miracle is a correction. It does not create, nor really change at all. It merely looks on devastation, and reminds the mind that what it sees is false. It undoes error, but does not attempt to go beyond perception, nor exceed the function of forgiveness.[6]**

Although a change of mind can and does sometimes *express* itself as a physical change we see right away in the world, it won't always happen that way, and the Course's focus is never about behavior or anything manifesting or changing in *form*.

A miracle, according to Ken Wapnick's *Glossary-Index for A Course in Miracles*, is "the change of mind that shifts our perception from the ego's world of sin, guilt, and fear, to the Holy Spirit's world of forgiveness" (Foundation for *A Course in Miracles*, Eighth Edition, 2018). It brings our focus from the body back to the mind. The miracle shows us who the dreamer is.

The Course is simple because all illusions are looked at and forgiven in the same way. An illusion is an illusion is an illusion!

> **There is no order of difficulty in miracles. One is not "harder" or "bigger" than another. They are all the same. All expressions of love are maximal.[7]**

When we go above the battleground to the decision-maker in our minds and shift our perception, we are reminded of two things: First, all problems in the world must come from the ego because their purpose is to distract us from the one and only problem: the mind's belief in *guilt*. Second, guilt itself is illusory because it comes from the illusory *belief* that we've sinned against God. If the separation from God never occurred, which is what the atonement principle tells us — that means there is no sin. If there's no sin then there's no reason to feel guilty, and no need to fear punishment. Therefore, there is no need to make up a world to hide in to escape punishment. We can forgive ourselves for choosing to believe the separation was real in the first place. Simple, right? Not easy! We're asked to question everything we have ever thought was true. We believe what others say and do in the world affects us. We can be led beyond this experience:

> **In reality you are perfectly unaffected by all expressions of lack of love.[8]**

The Course is not easy because all this is unconscious to us, and we find it hard to believe we made all this up! Jesus is re*mind*ing us we made an insane choice for the ego and have forgotten that choice.

To paraphrase Ken Wapnick, the miracle's function brings us back to the decision maker, the point of choice in the mind, so that we can view both dreams: The ego's dream of specialness as an individual, separate from our Creator, and the Holy Spirit's happy dream of forgiveness, where we know that what the ego made is insane and untrue. The miracle helps us contrast the two dreams — the two thought systems — and see the contrast from the observing mind. This is what will motivate us to allow its undoing when we're ready. This is why we're taught to look at our upsets with the Holy Spirit or Jesus as our teacher. We're only motivated to make a change when we don't like something the way it is.

Application to Our Everyday Lives

We go through all these senseless journeys, as Dorothy does, believing that our salvation lies in something or someone external. Finally, we realize we can turn the tables on the insanity of the ego. This is how we can experience inner peace no matter what is happening to us or around us.

Whenever we feel bad, angry, jealous, sad, or a victim of the world's circumstances, we remember (in our moment of crisis or mild upset) that we must be caught up in the false world of perception or else we wouldn't react to things as if they were real. In other words, we must have chosen the ego as our teacher. In that moment — stop! Remember you're dreaming and you can choose once again to view the Holy Spirit's script — the true forgiveness script where we remember that we can forgive what the body's eyes are showing us because what we're seeing isn't true.

Nothing so blinding as perception of form.[9]

Form is so blinding because we're seeing a world that isn't there. We're being deceived. Is Oz real? No, but Dorothy *believed* it was and reacted accordingly. When she woke up, it was gone. Why? Because it was made up. Where did it go? It disappeared because it was never there. Why? Because there's nothing outside the mind of the dreamer but a false projection made up by a false *thought* in the sleeping mind.

So, practically in the world, we live normal lives here; we just live under a different set of principles. We remember to forgive instead of judge when anything disturbs us. We have the willingness to see that we are dreaming instead of believing there are real people "out there" doing things to us. With the Holy Spirit's help, we begin to lessen our investment in physical sight in favor of spiritual sight or Christ's Vision. This is another way of seeing. It is not with the body's eyes. It's an awareness; an attitude that you have. People are really split off shadows of guilt projected from our own dreaming mind. Daily spiritual practice is using these projected images and circumstances in our life for the Holy Spirit's purpose instead of the ego's. His purpose is to gently correct our perception, awaken us and whisper that we are safe at home; we never left perfect oneness in Heaven. We learn to look past appearances and people's insane behavior to the mind's *content* of fear that's behind it. It is the same fear we all have while we appear to live in this world. This is how Jesus was appearing to be *in* the world, but not *of* it. He perceived correctly in his mind. He knew that what he was seeing was his own projection. The world was coming *from* him, not being done *to* him. His awareness was outside the holographic time-space dream. Our brothers and sisters are our saviors! We can't get home without them. We go home together or not at all. They are showing us our "state of mind" in every moment according to how we *think* about them. Jesus says to us:

> **Brother, you need forgiveness of your brother, for you will share in madness or in Heaven together. And you and he will raise your eyes in faith together, or not at all.[10]**

It's helpful to review what the world's purpose is and why we made a world of fragmentation. The world's purpose is to keep our separated selves intact. This is the ego's survival strategy:

> **Thus were specifics made. And now it is specifics we must use in practicing. We give them to the Holy Spirit, that He may employ them for a purpose which is different from the one we gave them.[11]**

The ego's wish is to find fault in these "specifics," which are everyone and everything in the world. Then we aren't responsible for our sin of choosing against God and wholeness in favor of a special self and separation. Jesus then says of the Holy Spirit:

> **Yet He can use but what we made, to teach us from a different point of view, so we can see a different use in everything**[12]

One of Gary Renard's teachers in DU, Pursah, says about our brothers:

> You should be grateful to them; you need them as much as they need you. Without those images you see and the miracle, you'd *never* be able to find the way out. These images are symbolic of what's in your unconscious mind and without them, your unconscious guilt would be forever hidden from you — there would be no escape.[13]

The Holy Spirit helps us recognize where the real cause of our discontent is — in the mind's choice for the ego — the teacher of discontent. Recognizing this and changing our perception is the miracle.

But I Don't Feel Guilty

When people say that they don't feel guilty and that they are having a good life, there is still unconscious guilt. Not everybody is ready to wake up and look at their judgments, much less tackle a thought system like the Course. It's nice to be viewing a relatively "good" lifetime DVD! Some people are not interested in a conscious spiritual path in this lifetime. However, the fact that they think they're a body actually living a life outside of Heaven means they *unconsciously* believe they're guilty, but the guilt been repressed. They're not in touch with it. Does it matter? No. That is, it is not an issue for a Course student. It is not necessary to proselytize for this thought system or any other and convince people that this way is the best way to inner peace and happiness. It is not necessary to correct people and point out, for example, that they are "in their ego." If I find myself about to correct someone in any way, I quickly recognize that I need the correction! Meaning, I choose to correct my *belief* about them in my mind and therefore not have to be right or defend a certain position with huge investment. This doesn't mean you won't have opinions and disagree with people. That's normal. What changes is that in your *mind* you won't *believe* you're separate from them. You'll know you are both part of the projection. With the Holy Spirit guiding your thoughts your responses won't be *reactionary* as if you have to make a point and be believed. You'll just make your point and not be invested in the other person believing you or agreeing with you. It can just be a normal, healthy discussion. You agree to disagree!

People will learn the truth when it's their time to do so, and in whatever way is helpful. *A Course in Miracles* is one path of many. It says that:

It is but one version of the universal curriculum. There are many others, this one differing from them only in form. They all lead to God in the end[14]

Remember: there's nothing wrong with living a good life here! But we won't undo our unconscious guilt if we believe it's *true*.

Thinking of People as They Really Are

It is no doubt unsettling at first when we start to integrate the Course's teaching that everything here is illusory, including all the bodies we see. It is natural to think that it's uncaring to think of people as unreal. What about our children? Parents? Things we love? It's not necessary to dive deeply into the metaphysics of the Course each time something upsets you. However, it is the template that eventually you want to keep in mind when you're ready to do so. ACIM would say that it's actually uncaring to think of anyone as *less* than what they really are — perfect Spirit.

Remember that to practice this thought system, you only have to be aware of which teacher you're choosing in your mind to guide you throughout your day. If you remember when someone upsets you that we are all really perfect Spirit having a dream of separation, then this is how you'll come to think of yourself — as perfect Spirit — because there is only one mind.

As you see him you will see yourself.[15]

This is true because your unconscious mind knows there's only one of us here. So it translates what you think about another to really be about you. You have normal relationships with your children as you're raising them. You have normal interactions with the people in your life. The difference is you can either come from love or fear *in your mind* no matter what roles you're engaged in. This difference is another key in the practice of true forgiveness.

When you remember to change your mind and think with the Holy Spirit, you'll *automatically* be kind and loving. You will automatically be compassionate and caring. You don't have to worry about what that *looks* like in each situation. The *content* of love in your mind will take the *form* that is most helpful in every situation. If you are focused on the content of love in your mind, the effect will take care of itself *without ego interference*. Yes, that means without *your* interference! This is hard for us! *We* want to decide what's best.

When you are stuck trying to make a decision you will remember that you have an inner teacher that has the answers. For example, if you are comforting someone who is suffering and wonder what to say to them, with the Holy Spirit in your mind you'll be thinking about them as perfect Spirit and your words or actions will flow *through* you from that thought. Remember — you will be normal in your activities, but you will know in your mind that you are not separate from the other person. So instead of the ego thought of "poor them" or

"I forgive them because I'm a better person or I'm a Christian or more evolved," you would be remembering that this is your dream and you know this is an opportunity to see it for what it is — a projection coming from you. You will *only* be kind, loving and helpful when following your right-minded teacher.

This awareness is done silently in your mind no matter what your body is guided to do. What your body does or does not do is not your concern. Whatever is done will be done *through* you when you take yourself out of the way. This is such a relief, because you're only becoming more of what you really are. When you're in the right mind you're only focused on the content of love in your mind. Your behavior will *extend* from that. Behavior is just the effect. What you do after switching your internal teacher will follow automatically and you won't worry about *what* to do. Your focus has become with *whom* you're doing it. This is not a minor distinction. This is another key to be aware of in your daily practice. It is a relief to let go and trust!

Change Your Mind's Default Setting

The default setting here in the world is the ego's perception. This is why we need the Holy Spirit's help. We cannot do this alone because we need help in making the right mind our default setting. This is what "looking" at our grievances with the Holy Spirit helps us do. Grievances stay put when they're not looked at. This is how forgiveness becomes a consistent attitude.

Instead of following the ego's direction automatically, the Holy Spirit starts to take over your mind and you are ready to forgive whatever comes up throughout the day, because you've already made the decision to put the right teacher in charge. To repeat, you are "miracle-ready" instead of "judgment-ready."

I have a saying that has been on my refrigerator for years. Whenever I'm upset I recite it to myself as a reminder: *"I made this and I am reacting to my own projection. I could see peace instead."* Then I remember to look at my upset with my right-minded teacher so He can show me a new interpretation of what I'm seeing. My upset is no longer a grievance I hold, but rather it is transformed into the miracle of Christ's Vision.

In short, it's impossible to forgive people for what they've done if we think it really happened. Inherent in the ego thought system is the belief that our life in the body is real (and often unfair) and things have indeed actually happened. That is how the ego *interprets* what the body's eyes see. When it's real to your mind, it keeps the thought of separation intact. It does not undo the unconscious guilt buried in your mind. Therefore, we truly "help" everyone and "save" the world by changing our *mind* about people and the world. By forgiving ourselves of our own unconscious guilt, we forgive people and "the world" because we are one with it. It is our projection. We're forgiving the contents of our own mind. Let's recall the projection together! We all go home together or no one goes home at all. It's important to not leave anyone out in your practice. If you leave one person out, it keeps the entire projection real.

Have you ever heard people say that forgiveness sets *you* free? This is true because when you forgive someone, you're lifting your faulty perception of them in favor of the truth about them. In doing this you offer it to yourself. Why? Because you're forgiving the contents of your own mind seen as many different people "out there." God's Son is one. Jesus is a *symbol* in our mind that serves as a reminder of this oneness. There is only one separated mind appearing as many.

Here are some helpful steps in practicing forgiveness from Lesson 23 in the Course's Workbook for Students. I've expanded on them here:

1. Whenever you're upset, sad, depressed or irritated, remember to stop in that moment. If you're feeling anything less than peaceful, pause in that moment. *The cause must be identified.* This is where we can revisit Lesson 5 which says, "I am never upset for the reason I think." I think I'm upset because of what someone said or did to me in the world, but what I'm seeing is only an outward pictorial representation of the choice for separation in my mind.

2. Remember you have two ways of perceiving what you're seeing. *We let go* of our interpretation of the problem. This is the second step. We ask Jesus to look at our guilt and attack thoughts

with us so we see them differently: my attack (judgment) on you was a made-up projection and the attack on myself was made-up too, because I never really separated from God. Therefore, I don't have to feel guilty and fear his punishment. The ego tells you the reason you're upset is because of what you're seeing with the body's eyes or perceiving with the senses. It further tells you that you have to do something about it, and the answer can only be found by some action taken in the world.

The Holy Spirit would have you look at the purpose you're giving the problem. He will remind you that you are the observer of the figures in the dream, including your own body that seems attached to you. His purpose is using the outward problem as a classroom for forgiveness, for true perception. The ego's purpose is always to separate and always stems from fear. Here is when you switch to the Holy Spirit's interpretation of what your senses have brought back to you. He uses everything for forgiveness. We can remember the body and the world were made by the ego to experience separation. That's why Jesus or the Holy Spirit helps us change our purpose for them. Under Their guidance we will use the body lovingly and kindly, without investment in a specific outcome that the ego tells us we need to be happy.

3. Trust the Holy Spirit and choose His strength. In the third step, *we let the ego thought system be replaced.* After we do steps one and two, we step back and let Him lead the way. This means we let Jesus' love in our right minds *reflect* through us here. We don't have to be the "doers," but rather allow a different thought system to be expressed *through* us as an extension of joining with the right mind. Remember, *A Course in Miracles* does not leave us hanging. It gives us a thought system to replace what we've made. *This point is so important because we won't feel like everything is meaningless, even though in Reality this is not our home.* The Course meets us where we are and helps us lift the veil slowly, so we can awaken without fear. We live normally — we enjoy our families, lives, and activities, but we change our internal teacher.

This makes things simple. Not easy to practice, but simple. We don't have to try to decide what outcome will be best, we don't have to feel good or bad, we can just be — knowing that changing our mind is our part in healing any situation. Our part is seeing shared interests; the shared interest in wanting to feel better because we're all afraid. The shared interest that we all separated at once and want to be home. You will automatically observe yourself taking action, but it will reflect the Holy Spirit's thought system instead of the ego's.

Letting go is not about being a doormat. It's about letting your right-minded teacher lead instead of the ego. You're active to the Holy Spirit and passive to the ego. This is leading from a peaceful place instead of a fearful one. Your response to people or circumstances could be anything from tough love to silence. It won't matter because you are only focused on the *content* of love in your mind: forgiveness instead of judgment, innocence instead of guilt, wholeness instead of separation, peace instead of pieces.

True forgiveness is the cornerstone of ACIM's teaching because it's what wakes you up! We are doing our normal activities here, but with our new teacher. As you forgive, huge shifts are taking place in your unconscious mind. We have to be willing to do our part and then the Holy Spirit takes care of the larger part we can't see. Our part is forgiving what comes up in our everyday life.

> **Forgiveness is the final illusion, as it forgives what never was, and leads beyond all illusion to the truth of God.[16]**

CHAPTER 4

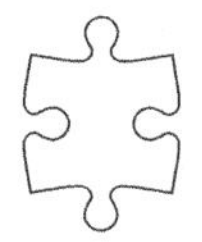

Our Life Scripts Are Written

> You can be in the wrong place at the wrong time, but you can be in the right mind ALL the time! — Jackie Lora Jones

> Happiness does not depend on outward things, but on the way we see them. — Leo Tolstoy

THE COURSE TEACHES that we are:

Reviewing mentally what has gone by.[1]

Dorothy's journey to Oz begins with her house swirling in a tornado. She is sitting up in bed watching her life scenes go by outside the window while unaware she is really asleep dreaming. Her window is like a screen and she's the observer. This is a fairly good metaphor for understanding the Course's teaching that we are merely watching past images (our life) go by on a movie screen in our *mind*, and our one remaining choice here is with whom we are going to watch the movie. The Holy Spirit or the ego? We are watching not as the body we're currently identified with, but as a dreaming mind, outside of time and space.

This was another important piece of the puzzle ACIM helped me put together. As I was using different manifesting techniques in my "spiritual buffet line" days, I noticed that while I manifested some things I wanted, I couldn't manifest other things. I wondered why that was so. Was I not doing it right? What was the difference between one thing and another? Did I not deserve to manifest a windfall of money or the perfect job?

I guess I was wondering, "If we're good at something and pursue it diligently with enthusiasm, why do we fall short and not end up getting what we want? Also, on the flip side, why is it often hard to pursue what we *think* we want?"

I remember in the late 90's I was working in a restaurant and taking acting classes here in Los Angeles. I felt somewhat guilty that I wasn't using my degree in broadcast journalism and working yet in that field. I had some fear about pursuing it. Something always stopped me from following through on a lead, and I would fall short. I was a great server, making a lot of money at a top restaurant. It was "safe," I thought. I had been practicing all my manifesting techniques and creative visualizations that Shakti Gawain and others at that time were writing about. I was also attracted to Wayne Dyer's book, *You'll See It When You Believe It: The Way to Your Personal Transformation* (William Morrow & Co, 1989).

That same year I was in acting class one evening, and I thought of my goal of wanting to help people in the world and wishing to contribute spiritually to the higher good. My intuition was telling me that acting wasn't the way I would do it. Journalism was my top interest, but I had somehow found myself temporarily swept up in the huge acting community here in Los Angeles. After all, in junior high and high school I loved my drama classes. One of my most joyful experiences was being cast as Brigitta in "The Sound of Music." In addition, I took dance throughout junior high and high school which brought me so much joy. I think I was on Broadway in a past life!

I was learning a lot in my acting workshops, and was told I was quite good, but my inner guidance was gently nudging me toward using my journalistic skills in this lifetime. After all, it's what I really wanted to do. I knew this growing up, so what happened? I got derailed. It wasn't the first time.

I followed my guidance and shifted my focus back to journalism. Oprah had just come out with new programming on *The Oprah Winfrey Show* called "Change Your Life TV." She was interviewing spiritual authors and teachers. "Finally," I thought. I hadn't seen it done before, but this was exactly what I envisioned myself doing. I told everyone, "You have to watch Oprah —

this new programming will be helpful to people." "Good," I thought. "She's doing it, so it's possible."

Not too long after that I stumbled upon an ad for a broadcasting class being offered at Santa Ana College in Santa Ana, CA. The thing that attracted me to this class was that a good portion of it was devoted to hands-on experience. We were actually going to be reporting the news for the college TV station. Not only would I get to be out in the field reporting on events, but I would have the opportunity to anchor real news segments in the studio.

As I had done several times before in my life, I followed the "hit," left acting class, and enrolled at the college. Once again, I felt so good! As soon as I stepped onto the news set and sat in the anchor chair, I felt at home. "What took me so long to get back to this?"

I remember the camera operator saying to me after my first newscast, "Wow that was great Jackie! How long have you been doing this?" I was stunned at first and answered him honestly, "I just started." I told him I had a degree in broadcast journalism from Indiana University in Bloomington, IN, but had not yet worked in the field.

I felt like broadcasting was as easy as breathing. It felt natural to me. I think the cameraman picked up on that, and thought I'd been doing it longer than I had been. I was reminded of another thing I "knew" growing up. My major in college was always going to be broadcast journalism. I never had a doubt. Interesting that I didn't pursue it consistently with determination after college. I did apply for a position or two, but didn't get the jobs. It wasn't in the cards. Why? I wondered. Here's why my sought-after jobs weren't in the cards:

Not in the Script

We won't always manifest the things we *think* we want. We often feel guilty about getting derailed for whatever reason, and "wasting time," but we only see one piece of the puzzle. In retrospect it was a blessing I didn't get those jobs. It would have put me on an undesired path.

The Course is teaching that our life scripts are written. Everything that is going to happen has indeed already happened. It says:

> **Time is a trick, a sleight of hand, a vast illusion in which figures come and go as if by magic. Yet there is plan behind appearances that does not change. The script is written. When experience will come to end your doubting has been set. For we but see the journey from the point at which it ended, looking back on it, imagining we make it once again; reviewing mentally what has gone by.**[2]

When Jesus says, "...The script is written. When experience will come to end your doubting has been set," he is reminding us that the time when we want to stop experiencing pain and suffering is *already* there as a script in the mind. This is the script when we can actually awaken fully from the dream. Awakening from the dream is enlightenment in the Course.

Because we are dreaming our lives here as a dreaming mind, watching one of the many scripts or movies that have *already been filmed*, the mind is either viewing one of two sets of scripts all the time: the ego's script of guilt and punishment or the Holy Spirit's script of forgiveness and healing. Ken Wapnick uses this analogy:

> Imagine the sleeping Son of God sitting in front of a television screen, with a VCR [or DVD] perched on top. On either side of the set are two almost infinitely large libraries of video tapes, filled with different aspects of fear and forgiveness respectively. The Son, asleep in his mind *outside time*, chooses which video tape he will experience, which dream he will have. Once making that choice, it seems to him that he is actually experiencing that video drama, when in truth he is merely re-experiencing what has *already* happened.[3]

So when Jesus tells us the script is written, he is talking about this library of scripts to choose from that have *already* happened. The Course teaches that the world was over long ago. The ego's script of sin, guilt and fear was projected out of the mind into a world of our *seeming* life scripts. This happened all at once. All ego scripts are occurring simultaneously within a fixed system. We can switch dimensions of time as a result of our forgiveness, but we're still in the illusion. The Holy Spirit's correction scripts of forgiveness also happened at the same time. Remember ACIM's story of the Big Bang? Ken Wapnick continues:

> Remember that the entire movie *including* the correction has already been filmed, and encompasses the world of evolution, spanning billions of years....Thus, we are as observers sitting in front of a screen watching what has already taken place, as if it were occurring for the first time. Our *experience*, however, is that we are actually part of what we are observing.[4]

No one is denying that we're having the *experience* that we're in control of *what* happens here in the world, but the Course tells us that isn't the case. If there's no world out there, then there are no bodies to inhabit it. So how could we be making things happen right now as a body?

The Holy Spirit's forgiveness scripts are also part of the illusion, but instead of furthering illusions they lead us out of them. They recall the projection, so to speak. The Holy Spirit's scripts are the ego's scripts seen through the lens of forgiveness. By choosing the Holy Spirit's forgiveness scripts we slowly awaken from the dream.

This is a process. We don't just wake up and go poof all at once! It would frighten us. We first change our nightmare dreams of fear and separation into "happy dreams" of forgiveness before awakening to oneness with God. When the Course talks about the happy dream, the happy dream is still in the mind of the dreamer and still part of the illusion. However, it is a gentler dream as we are allowing the Holy Spirit to undo our unconscious guilt through forgiveness and the miracle. The power of true forgiveness and the miracle enables us to see our brothers and sisters differently, and to undo the belief that God will punish us.

We are undoing the idea of the false self in our minds. We start to see everyone as the same. Not because bodies are the same, but rather, we know that they are not really bodies and they, too, have a right-mind, a wrong mind, and the ability to choose which teacher to follow. We see our shared interests of wanting the peace of God. We all forgot as the one collective mind that we chose the ego on another level. This is how we *think* about everyone we encounter, regardless of what their behavior is showing us.

We can identify with the reflection of Heaven's truth by choosing the Holy Spirit's forgiveness script whenever we're afraid, angry, depressed or unhappy. That's why Jesus says "choose once again." After all, the only reason we feel bad is because we've chosen to view the ego's scripts of sin, guilt and fear, and part of that choice is believing they are our reality. We believe that on this level, as a body, we are making choices here. In actuality, real choice is only made at the mind level, and there are only two choices: love or fear, innocence or guilt, forgiveness or judgment, wholeness or separation. Changing our internal teacher from the ego to the Holy Spirit and mentally reviewing His correction scripts precedes our awakening.

Much more can be offered for further understanding of ACIM's explanation of our life scripts and the illusion of linear time, which is beyond the scope of this book. My goal for Book One of *The Wisdom Series™* is to introduce the Course's teaching that our identity in the illusion is as the observer in the dreaming mind, not the body, and to illustrate that it is unnecessary to worry if you strive to manifest things here and some manifest and some don't. There's a reason for it!

The Course is teaching us that our true happiness depends on how we *look* at our life, not *what* happens in it. We are not controlling what happens to ourselves and others on this level, although we believe we are. We chose our scripts on another level when we chose to believe in separation instead of unity, fragmentation instead of wholeness. I will expand on this in future books in this series. I recommend Ken Wapnick's book, *A Vast Illusion: Time according to A Course in Miracles* (Foundation for *A Course in Miracles*, Third Edition, 2006) for an in-depth look and great clarity on this topic.

With that said, we would all agree that certain scenarios *seem* better than others in the world. There is no reason to deny that. The ego would have it no other way than to make levels in this illusion where some people seem better off than others. Let's take money for example. It's easier to live when you have money than when you do not. To bodies, this is obvious. However, when we're *invested* and dependent on anything external for our *salvation*, we will often be disappointed. The world is set up to keep us in lack *somehow*. More importantly, the ego wants us to keep chasing happiness in the world. Why? Because then we'll never learn it's an illusion we made up, and we'll never go back to the mind and discover what the true *cause* of our distress is — the choice for the ego. When we choose the ego we're "making the error real," Jesus teaches us. The error is *believing* that we can actually be separate and have an existence apart from our oneness in Heaven.

Keeping in mind that the entire world of time and space is an illusion, both scenarios (having money or not having money) are equally untrue. With this reminder, we can understand why the focus of ACIM is always on changing our *mind* about our situation. Then that new choice for Jesus or the Holy Spirit will inform our decisions and actions here. For example, when we look at our financial situation differently with our new teacher of forgiveness instead of the ego's fear, we may feel more relaxed about it for the moment. Then from a more relaxed state we may get inspired to see a new way to add to our income. Something just "hits" us out of the blue. The counsel of ACIM is always to change your internal teacher first when you're anything less than peaceful. Then your actions follow your new thought — the new thought being a forgiveness thought. This thought lets you know that you are not a body, but rather a dreaming mind. Your new teacher will be the navigator of your thinking throughout the rest of your time here. This is the first step. You can do it! It just takes practice! It will change your *experience* of your life for sure. Sometimes your external situation will change too, even though that's not the focus of *A Course in Miracles.*

To make an important point, there's nothing wrong with having preferences and wanting to manifest things in your life here. Everyone wants to have a better life, and it's built into the script that we are indeed able to manifest certain things. Think of it like a game! Have fun with it if you want to! But do you have to be invested in it as your *salvation*? Do you have to believe it's true? Just be normal and do the things you would normally do, but do them with a different teacher in your mind. That will not only help you feel better, but you'll become more peaceful, be helpful to other minds that are in fear, and start to wake up to a bliss and joy that we can't imagine. Staying rooted in the ego thought system will never be the answer that will give you permanent peace and happiness. As soon as you manifest something that makes you happy, there will be something else you want or need! Or, what you previously manifested doesn't turn out to bring you the happiness you thought it would! It's an endless search because nothing will ever satisfy us and be able to substitute for the love of God and being home in Heaven.

The Course is teaching that *what* happens in our individual life and the world will not always change to our liking, but we can change the way we *look* at what's happening in the world. This is what wakes us up to what we *really* want — the uninterrupted consistency of inner joy and peace of mind no matter what is happening. The shift from the ego's videos to the Holy Spirit's videos is not a shift in form, meaning the body and the world. It's a shift in the *mind* to our right-minded teacher that holds the loving memory that everything is okay and we are loved. The Holy Spirit's gentle guidance reminds us that we don't have to believe in our silly made-up nightmare dreams.

> **There is no point in trying to change the world. There is no point in trying to change the script. It is incapable of change because it's merely an effect. But there is indeed a point in changing your thoughts about the world. Here you are changing the cause. The effect will change automatically.[5]**

Thus we can be in the right mind *all the time*, even if what our eyes are showing us is not so great at any given moment. When we're truly in our right mind, we won't believe the dream is true. We'll continue with all our different roles here, but we'll know we're dreaming. That's the miracle. My sister Cindy and I will often call each other and say, "I'm really feeling the dream right now." We laugh. She knows what I mean when I call her and I know what she means when she calls me. It's an experience, not anything that can be explained in words, so we rarely try. We just know. I would offer, though, that everything is lighter, you look past appearances, time kind of runs together and is blurred, there's a feeling of detachment (in a good way), eyes are quiet; there's a gentle smile.

From this perspective we can look at everything differently. Do you see? We are undoing the separation idea in our mind in favor of joining with others in our shared interest of waking up from the dream. The right-minded interpretation is one of peace. This is why we are happy. We remember the truth.

Again, there's nothing wrong with wanting to meet our needs here and have a nice life. Enjoy your life when enjoyment is happening in the script! Why wouldn't you? The Course has nothing against that. It is asking us whenever we are upset and can't seem to get what we *think* we want, to remember that we're being fooled into thinking things in the world will satisfy us instead of the peace and love of God. It's reminding us to choose a different teacher. We can have a different *experience* of our lives here, no matter what is happening in our script at the moment. Thus, we can be in the right mind *all the time*, even if we are watching a painful event happen or experiencing pain and strife in our life or the world at large.

Looking with the Holy Spirit Instead of the Ego

I didn't know about the two choices back in the 90's when I felt guilty about not pursuing my "chosen major" wholeheartedly after college. Had I known what the *real* problem was, I would have had a different *experience*. I was trying to make the dream better and figure it all out on my own. I had been watching the ego's tapes and therefore felt I was Jackie, who was a person feeling guilty for not pursuing my college major in the way the world teaches we should. Consequently, I was under the impression that I as Jackie could have done better. I felt the accompanying feelings of unworthiness and failure at times. This is because this is what I wanted to feel on another level. Everything here in dreamland can be used for either the Holy Spirit's or the ego's purpose. In the early 90's I used the situation of not getting a job for the ego's purpose — to feel unfairly treated, that I was somehow unworthy or inferior. This kept me focused on the illusory problem.

Underlying all that was the hidden unconscious satisfaction that I usurped the power of God and claimed my "special" individual self. We unconsciously believe we pulled off the impossible and secretly want this to be true. In addition, the ego told us we could get rid of the guilt we feel through projection.

Now when I begin my day, I put the Holy Spirit in charge. This way my *purpose* has changed. I set the goal to remember the truth at the beginning of the day. Then, whatever happens is used as the *means to achieve that goal.* Everything that comes up during my day will be used to experience inner peace and inclusion, not suffering and separation. My new interpretation of not getting a job would be that "I" don't have to take that personally. If I'm not a body, does it matter if I get a certain job or not? No, it doesn't. If I take it personally it serves the ego's goal which is to prove I'm an innocent victim and the world is doing me wrong. This reaffirms the choice for separation in the mind.

What I *do* with what happens becomes my new script, meaning how I *experience* what happens will change when choosing the right-minded teacher. The ego's purpose for all the happenings would have me believing they're true, keeping me stuck in sin, guilt and fear. Instead, the Holy Spirit's purpose reinterprets what happens through the power of forgiveness.

Instead of feeling guilty about what I was doing or not doing, I would've remembered that I could choose to see my situation through the Holy Spirit's interpretation. I would see that I'm not really unfocused and not pursuing things enough, but that I'm *dreaming* that I'm a body that appears unfocused or appears to not pursue things in the way that the world dictates. I would have remembered that my identity in the dream is not a body, but a dreaming mind capable of waking up at any time. Then I wouldn't have remained in the sin, guilt and fear script, but would have switched to the forgiveness script or video and had peace no matter *what* the outcome. This is how we undo the false self.

The point of time when I eventually returned to journalism would have still happened, but I would not have had the guilt and suffering before my return. *That's* the forgiveness script. I would have changed my *mind* about my life instead of feeling guilty as a real person *in* it. Maybe something would have changed in form by practicing forgiveness, but maybe it wouldn't have. What *would* have definitely changed was my experience.

I look back now and realize I couldn't have been anywhere else on my journey but where I was at the time. I was viewing an ego movie that had already been filmed, was over long ago, and never actually happened in reality anyway. This awareness puts the pieces together!

In summary, our identity in the dream is of a dreaming mind that observes and chooses. Our last remaining choice here is *with whom* we are going to watch the movie of our life. The Course teaches we can watch with the ego, which will tell us we're the figure *in* the dream and at the mercy of all its effects of sin, guilt and fear. Or we can watch with the Holy Spirit or Jesus and be reminded that we're dreaming and that nothing really happened in Reality. When we watch with the Holy Spirit we've chosen His interpretation of our dream. That is what the Course calls the "happy dream of forgiveness." They're not happy dreams because everything in the *script* is happy. They're happy because we're viewing the happenings and circumstances of our lives with the correction script, where we are reminded we did not sin, we are not really guilty and we don't deserve punishment. Our actions flow *through* us instead of feeling like we *need* to do something.

With regard to being disappointed in the early 90's by not getting a certain job, and feeling like I wasn't pursuing the right career path and therefore wasting time, I would now recognize that it was a trick of the ego in order to keep me in the world as a body and away from my real identity in the illusion as a dreaming mind. My guilt over my perceived inadequacy remained intact then. Now, I know to forgive those thoughts and feelings of inadequacy, allowing my unconscious guilt to be healed by the Holy Spirit each time I am anything less than peaceful.

I now see any bad feelings in any situation as an opportunity to wake up from my dream. The problem wasn't that there was anything wrong with me because I didn't get a certain job. The *real* problem was that I thought I was a body at all. I did not know I was dreaming and watching a life script play out. I was invested in having my life be a certain way, resisting the present moment. I put my self-worth and salvation into getting the right job and having people be proud of me and my accomplishments. I thought the situation was real. We still believe the world is real right now when we get triggered, right? Again, it's okay to want to do well and be your best. Why wouldn't you want that? That's normal. We'll feel our best when we allow the love in our minds to guide our thoughts.

Further, I now know that whenever something happens that I don't like or if I feel inadequate in any way, that the ego has those scenarios scripted out *already*. If I continue to believe I am a body, I fall into the trap of feeling not good enough, not helpful enough, or that I don't deserve to manifest something. Tricky ego! The Holy Spirit would say, "What body?"

Again, no one is denying that we need to have jobs here in the world, but do we have to put our *salvation* in them? Changing our mind and waking up from the illusion doesn't mean we aren't doing normal things here: earning a living, raising children, having relationships and so forth. The difference is that we're not *invested* in what happens, as we learn to *trust* that the Holy Spirit knows what's best for everyone involved and will guide us to that outcome if we get ourselves out of the way! The Holy Spirit assures us that all is well and if we just listen to His Voice, we will have all the answers we need. All our problems are easily solved because everything in the illusion is looked at and forgiven *in the same way*. Why? Because none of it is true.

If I feel upset, judged, or fearful these days, I automatically look on it with the Holy Spirit as my teacher and use the situation as a classroom for forgiveness. I shift from *what* is happening to remembering *why* I'm really upset. It's never for the reason I think. If the above example happened today I would say to myself, "Don't be fooled into thinking you are the body and there's something wrong with you because you didn't get that job. I know it's the guilt in my mind over the seeming separation that's the *real* problem. I am willing to see this job situation differently knowing that I don't choose to further illusions. There is no Jackie and no job out there really, so I can switch to the Holy Spirit's script and forgive my projected images (the images in this case are me as Jackie having a personal identity, and my belief that there's a job out there to get or not get)." Then I go to the next step of taking responsibility for dreaming my dream. I now have peace because I'm not guilty. Since there's no separation, I remember I'm really at home in Heaven; I just forgot for a moment. I can now lead my "normal" life, but under the guidance of my right mind. That is how I can be *truly* helpful here. It works! It feels good to remember the truth. When I remember the truth, I join with everyone's right mind, given that there's only one mind.

That's an example of how I practice forgiveness. We have to look at what upsets us in thought or feeling and allow the Holy Spirit to reinterpret what the body's eyes are showing us. This is how we can have inner peace no matter what is happening. We feel peaceful knowing nothing has happened in reality, just in our mistaken dreams. Why do we have to take everything so seriously? Only the ego does. Every upset or grievance has one solution — correct your perception about it because nothing is happening in an illusion. God is the only Reality.

Will we continue on in life to the best of our abilities in the dream? Of course, why wouldn't we? When we're coming from the right mind everything is easier. We will naturally do our best in our roles and be kind to others. Don't we function better with less guilt and conflict in the mind? As more and more conflict is removed from our minds we're free to just *be* and follow the guidance of our new inner teacher. The choice for our right-minded teacher will inform all our decisions and actions in the world. Is it really that simple? Yes! Is it easy to change our faulty perception? No! This is why we can't do it alone and why we use every grievance we hold as an opportunity to go back to the mind. We must have that "little willingness" to look at our judgments with Jesus and He will take care of the rest. He will heal the larger part of the mind that we can't see. Our job is to forgive whatever comes up in our lives every day. We're never deprived of our forgiveness opportunities!

The difference in my life today is that when the psychological pain of guilt, disguised as inadequacy shows up, I can laugh at it and remember the ego is using this situation to convince me I am a body, deeply flawed and inadequate in some way. The answer to my feeling of inadequacy and unworthiness cannot come from changing something out there on my screen. It has to come from within — from the source. Incidentally, when you've been practicing forgiveness for many years, it doesn't mean that you won't ever have bad thoughts or judgmental thoughts, you just won't react to them and indulge them in the same way. You'll come to a place of peace automatically, pretty quickly if not instantaneously. That's one sign the Holy Spirit is taking over your mind.

A tranquil mind is not a little gift[6]

Our only responsibility is which teacher do we choose; then the love in our minds will *reflect* through us and express itself in whatever form is most helpful.

How it extends through us is not our responsibility. We are not the "doers." Everything is done *through* us. We are in the world, but not *of* it. This is how we live in simplicity.

We live in peace, not pieces!

CHAPTER 5

If the World's an Illusion, What Is My Purpose Here?

> **The overlooking of the battleground is now your purpose. Be lifted up, and from a higher place look down upon it. From there will your perspective be quite different. Here in the midst of it, it does seem real.[1]**

THE WICKED WITCH of the West in *The Wizard of Oz* repeatedly sabotages Dorothy's journey. She tries to thwart the final approach to Oz's castle by putting a spell on a poppy field Dorothy must pass through. The spell causes Dorothy and some of her companions to fall asleep. They are fooled because the poppies are so pleasing to the eye; yet they have a nefarious purpose behind them. This is what the ego does. The ego tries to keep us asleep and dreaming, while tricking us into thinking we're going to get the prize. We are continuously tempted (with the carrot and stick approach) to find our happiness in external things, only to recognize that things aren't what they seemed to be. Once I get the job I want, I have a terrible boss or have to work long hours. Once I get the spouse I want, we seem to have endless arguments and don't see things the same way. Once I'm making more money, it goes to unexpected household repairs or hospital bills.

However, Glinda, the Good Witch of the North, wakes Dorothy by making it snow. This is a good metaphor for what the Holy Spirit does — helps us awaken from the dream. The Course teaches that the Holy Spirit doesn't do anything *in* the world, but He is in our *mind,* helping us remember the truth that the separation has not occurred. Choosing His thought system can show up in some *form or symbol* in the world that is helpful; that form being a *reflection* of our right-minded choice.

We naturally think of our purpose in the world in terms of career, philanthropic work, raising a family, or all of the above. We want to make sure we're using our gifts and talents, that we are making a contribution of some kind, making a living, and not wasting time, or not feeling like we're missing out. A common thought in the New Age movement is that we want to do what our heart desires. All the while, the ego succeeds in keeping us focused on finding our salvation *in* the world.

We endlessly chase after goals and dreams and it makes us crazy when things don't work out in our favor.

ACIM teaches that our only true function here is forgiveness; seeing with true perception. We think our function is all these other things in the world, such as our many roles. This is an effective ego distraction because we never feel that we're doing our best. There's always a feeling that there's more to do. In the past, I would think to myself, "I'm not there yet" or "There's something else I can still do."

To be sure, of course we want to be our best as a parent, a friend, in our careers and as responsible citizens. Why wouldn't we? When we listen to the Holy Spirit, we would *only* be kind, helpful and the best we could be in *all of our roles*. The problem is, we are listening to the ego most of the time and therefore are coming from a place of lack and scarcity, following a script where we *experience* guilt and fear punishment. Often we hope to look good and be successful in the eyes of others in order to feel accepted and worthy. The ego succeeds in keeping our focus on our reputation, our body and what the body does as the means of our salvation.

Listening to the Holy Spirit, on the other hand, would allow our gifts, talents and abilities to be expressed *through* us with no worry about how it looks and no investment in the outcome. The Holy Spirit guides us as to what is best for *all*, because He reminds us that there's really only one of us that seemed to separate from wholeness. Our salvation is never found in how others evaluate us or how we evaluate ourselves externally. The ego has set up our life scripts so we are never permanently satisfied! We are quite hard on ourselves and others.

Not being invested in the outcome doesn't mean we don't care. It means that we develop *trust* in our inner teacher who knows what's best for all concerned: ourselves, our children, our friends, our co-workers, as well as the world at large. When we're invested, it not only keeps us stuck in the ego's mess, but it makes the world real to our minds, keeps us suffering and delays our awakening.

Jesus is reminding us in ACIM that we are watching a projection we call our life. Our choice here is, "Which teacher are we going to watch our life movie with?" If we think we are the body and ignore the mind that made it, it will be impossible to be at peace. You will feel your life is in pieces. It will be literally in pieces because you'll be focused on separation, that is, all the different fragments that make up the illusory world.

The Course's uncompromising focus is not on *what* is happening to you, but how you're *looking* at it. Which interpretation of the dream will you choose while you're doing all the normal things you're doing here? The choice for the ego will keep you stuck in a make-believe world of separation, scarcity, lack, attack and judgment. The choice for the Holy Spirit will remind you that you made up this world and can awaken from your dream. You learn that God is a loving God instead of a punishing one, and what He creates is perfect Oneness. Then you can *practically apply* the reflection of this awareness by looking at your life through the lens of His love, which is the forgiveness script.

The ego analyzes; the Holy Spirit accepts.[2]

We spend an enormous amount of time trying to figure out what something means in the world. "Is it a sign?" we ask. It is also very common to analyze *why* something happens to us. For example, why did I get sick? Why didn't I get this job? Why didn't this relationship work out? What's the meaning in this situation?

While these are all good questions, and we certainly should take care of ourselves and our bodies to the best of our abilities, *A Course in Miracles'* focus is not on what happened and why it happened, but with *whom* am I looking at this? If our scripts are already written and we are merely reviewing mentally what has already gone by, why would we still believe that the body itself can make something "new" happen now? Whatever you see happening as "new" has already happened. Remember — you are mentally reviewing life scripts that have already happened and you're merely choosing to re-experience the fear-based scripts when you're in the ego mind.

When we switch our internal teacher, we switch to the Holy Spirit's forgiveness script and our *experience* gets easier. This is how we gently awaken. What has been scripted out for us does not have a hold on us in the same way. Think of something that happened to you 20 years ago. Does it still have the same hold on you? Most likely it seems more distant and you're not bothered by it in the same way. This is a feeling that can be more of your experience each and every day. Not because you're ignoring something or trying not to look at the pain, but because you're recognizing that you're dreaming and you can deny the ego's interpretation of the events in favor of *looking* with true perception. We must look at our upsets and issues to bring them to the light of truth. This is how the Holy Spirit takes over your mind. You start to lose investment in physical sight in favor of Spiritual sight. Seeing with Christ's Vision is not seeing with the body's eyes. It is interpreting through right minded perception which looks beyond the body and world; beyond the error of separation to the truth of Oneness.

In other words, you can change your mind about things that have happened to you; you can change your interpretation of your circumstances. Changing your mind means you recognize that these are events happening in a dream, so there's no use in worrying endlessly. Jesus says in the Course:

> **What worry can beset the one who gives his future to the loving Hands of God? What can he suffer? What can cause him pain or bring experience of loss to him? What can he fear? And what can he regard except with love?[3]**

I experience present peace when I remember to forgive my upsets as they occur. I know that the world has no power over me and cannot be a threat. I can't change something that's already happened. I can, however, change the *purpose* my mind has given it. There is a use in *looking* at the world differently and forgiving it. This wakes you up! This is your real purpose if your goal is awakening from your dream and having inner peace during the process.

The Paralysis of Analysis

The reason we overanalyze is because we think we have control of our lives from *within* the dream as a body and we want to have control over what happens next. We have forgotten that we made the choice for separation already, which is why we're even seeing a "world" we think is outside of us. Therefore, the only question to ask here is "Am I now looking at my life through the lens of conflict or the lens of peace?" While the mind is asleep and dreaming, our real life in Heaven has continued uninterrupted.

This is why the Course is simple. There are only two choices as you go through your life. It's not easy to practice! What passes for spirituality in parts of the New Age movement is analyzing *what* happens and either focusing on how to change it into something better or make sure it doesn't snowball into something worse! For example, our internal dialogue might say, "I got in a fender bender because I was not supposed to make it to my doctor's appointment because Jesus is saying that this doctor is not the right one for me. It's a sign." Okay, nothing wrong with that. But now you're left having to figure out who the right doctor would be and why. What if the new one isn't the right one either? And the next? Is the diagnosis correct? What about the right treatment?

To be sure, no one is saying that we shouldn't follow what we feel is a sign coming from our right mind, and we do get *inspired* ideas and "hits." I follow hits a lot. The problem arises when we make circumstances, events and our bodies real by overanalyzing, investing, and putting our *salvation* in things here. Is your salvation in making sure you're following the right signs? This makes the whole world real to your mind, therefore reinforcing the illusion and keeping your unconscious guilt intact.

Lastly, signs from "the other side" (meaning from loved ones that have passed on for example) are still part of the ego thought system because there is no other side. It's still all in the mind. It's still a separation idea that we make real, namely, that there's "you" who is receiving the information, and then there's "something or someone else" (other than you) giving you information. There's nothing right or wrong about following signs. It's fun to get signs! I receive messages from people who have passed. I follow inspired "pings" that come into my mind. This is being normal. We can be "inspired" here. If we remember our true identity and feel peaceful in the process, we know we're following our right mind. We wouldn't get signs if they weren't already scripted out for us. I follow the ones that resonate with me without attachment to what happens. My salvation is not dependent on a particular thing happening or not. If something turns out to be different that I thought, I'm not rattled by it. This is key in not making what happens real to your mind and therefore reinforcing illusions.

When you're in the right mind, you can follow what you believe to be signs without investment that they produce what you think they should produce for you. As soon as you're attached or disappointed in any way — the ego got you! Why? Because if you're dependent on a particular outcome to ensure peace or happiness, you've just put your salvation in an illusion. There's nothing wrong with having preferences and hoping for a particular outcome; but can you hope for it and then let it go into the Holy Spirit's hands so He can remind you of your true peace and happiness, regardless of what may or may not manifest in form? This is key.

There is no doubt my experience is better when I listen to my intuition and don't try to do things on my own. My hope in writing about this is to convey that the ego can be really tricky! You'll think it's the Holy Spirit's Voice when it's really the ego sneaking in the back door, masquerading as your savior. This time the right diet will work. This time I'll manifest the right relationship or job. This is the approach that will work with my kids. This time it'll be different. Sometimes we get too wrapped up in waiting for signs and we put immense investment in *what* happens — all to the ego's delight! Trust the Holy Spirit. It's what will bring you peace and joy. Jesus reminds us that the experience of God's love is what we *really* want.

He reminds us we can have whole song, meaning the peace of God. However, we are endlessly focused on effects and ask for specific signs and specific things in prayer.

> **You cannot, then, ask for the echo. It is the song that is the gift. Along with it come the overtones, the harmonics, the echoes, but these are secondary.[4]**

In summary, like anything else, we do the normal thing in the world. For me that means being grateful for signs I feel are *reflections* from my right mind. The key is to not be overly invested or become dependent on certain outcomes. Things won't turn out the way you want them to *every* time. However, the scripts are set up so that following "inspired" ideas and signs can lead to positive results on the level of form. With continued practice you'll be viewing the forgiveness script more of the time. This means you'll have peace in your mind *regardless* of what's happening on the level of the body and the world. Enjoy it!

For instance, when we go to see a movie in the theater, the cashier isn't standing at the ticket booth saying "Don't enjoy it; it's not real!" We can enjoy the movie in the theater. It's entertainment! So too, can we enjoy our life here when enjoyment is called for. Remember to be normal, as Ken Wapnick often said. After all, no one would deny that our lives here can be very entertaining, but so are our dreams at night. That doesn't make them *real.*

How I Practice in Everyday Life

It changes things when we start to awaken to the fact that this world is not our true home. At first, this awareness can be unsettling because this world is all we know.

A common question I receive is, "What do I do now? What's the point of anything?" The simple answer is that we "be normal" in the world, but live under a different set of principles: forgiveness instead of judgment, shared interests instead of separate interests, reflecting love instead of fear, innocence instead of guilt, joy instead of sorrow. This is how we start. The reason it's important to be normal is because if you're trying too hard to be "spiritual," it's making the world real to your mind because you're "trying" and "invested" in doing things right. We do what we would normally do, but when we're upset for any reason, *we notice and then change our internal teacher.* We would not be upset unless we first chose the teacher of upset; the ego. This means we must be making the world real and very important, or else we would not be upset. When we're upset is when we're asked to look at things differently, because that's when we're motivated to make a change — when something is not how we wish it to be. Who is the one who is wishing something were different? The false self.

Be with People Where They Are

In my work as a practicing therapist and spiritual counselor, I work with a wide variety of Course students who specifically want mentoring on the Course's perspective and how they can apply the teachings in their lives. I also have clients who know nothing about the world being an illusion. I am often reminded that all of us are exactly where we are supposed to be on our respective journeys.

First, I have people who talk to me about living their best life now because this life is all there is. They're not aware of dreaming or anything about the illusory nature of the world. That's fine. They are where they're supposed to be. Second, I have clients and friends who are excited to share their awareness of their past lives and how they've learned from them. Many talk about their mystical experiences: astral travel, messages they receive from angels and their deceased loved ones, extra-terrestrial contact, and so on. They also are right where they're supposed to be. Third, I have clients who understand that this is not their *real* identity. They specifically want to deepen their Course practice and awaken from the dream. They are exactly where they're supposed to be. The whole spectrum is represented, and everything in between.

I point this out to illustrate how I'm being normal in the world in my role as a therapist. It doesn't matter where anyone is on the awareness spectrum. People learn what they learn whenever they choose to learn it.

I'm still doing my *normal* job as a therapist helping people with the issues that are important to them. I help everyone wherever they are on the awareness spectrum. My job as a Course student is to not see them as separate from me. This is an attitude, done in the mind. It's how I'm *thinking* about them. I put the Holy Spirit in charge of every session so that any suggestions I offer are inspired — coming from the loving kindness of the right mind.

In other words, it doesn't matter *what* I'm doing here, or where people are on the awareness spectrum, but, rather, with *whom* am I looking at the dream? Am I, as a therapist, seeing clients as separate from me or not?

My function as a therapist is to be with people where they are and help them accordingly. I join with them *in my mind* and know there is really no separation between us; no client and therapist, no teacher and student. It is how I'm *thinking* about my clients that is the real healing. I think of them as perfect Spirit. Healing takes place in the mind. The right words for each client flow through my right-minded choice and I don't have to worry about what to say or do. Obviously different suggestions are given to different people. How would "I" know, as Jackie, what's best for any particular client in any given moment? What I do know is to make sure the ego is out of the way. Whatever I say or do will *reflect* love when I'm coming from my right mind. Yes, I use my natural skill sets and therapeutic techniques I learned in school, but I use them under the guidance of the Holy Spirit. This is the difference.

You can practice true forgiveness in any job, at any place, and at any time. It is not our function to point out the ego in others and police the universe. It is our job to wake up from our dream that there *is* a universe.

It is comforting to know that we can fulfill our true purpose of forgiveness here in any role. Forgiveness only has to do with the *content* in your mind, not the *form* your life takes. The content is either love - the Holy Spirit's right- minded thoughts that you reflect into your roles here, or fear - the ego's wrong- minded thoughts wanting you to live in guilt and fear because you believe you're a body that has sinned, feels guilty, and deserves punishment.

No matter what we are doing, we want to remember to be active to the Holy Spirit and passive to the ego. Being active to the Holy Spirit means we choose to look at our life as a classroom where we have endless opportunities for forgiveness. Our new challenge is to become aware of whether we've chosen the ego or the Holy Spirit. Our experience tells us which teacher we've chosen in any given moment. We know that whenever we are not at peace, we have chosen the ego and can choose once again. This is how it's possible to be at peace no matter *what* is happening around you. Nothing can take away the peace of God from you unless you've given it permission to do so. This is the practice of true forgiveness — recognizing that our outer world is only a projection of an inner choice. Our goal is to remember we are the producer of the play, not the figure in the play. We learn to use the body lovingly by recognizing it responds only to the intentions of the mind.

When we allow the Holy Spirit to guide our days we are not "reactive" and are not taken in by appearances.

> **Appearances deceive *because* they are appearances and not reality. Dwell not on them in any form. They but obscure reality, and they bring fear *because* they hide the truth.[5]**

With the Holy Spirit in our mind we relate to others in a gentler way. This doesn't mean we're excusing bad behavior or being a doormat. Rather, we remember what the *source* of the bad behavior is — fear. We know *in our mind* that it's only happening in a dream and we can choose to change our interpretation of situations before responding. With continued practice, this becomes an automatic attitude, a way of being. This new awareness will not further illusions, but wake us up from them. A major benefit is that you'll have a much better *experience* of your life.

Not being reactive allows for gentler right-minded thoughts to lead the way. These new thoughts will be forgiveness thoughts, reminding us that everyone we meet has a right mind, a wrong mind and the ability to choose between them. In our new way of relating to people, we know they are either calling out for love or expressing love. People call out for love in the most horrific ways, for sure. However, our response in *thought* to all our brothers is love. *Remember that what you're seeing never left your mind and so you can change your mind about it.* This is choosing the miracle. A miracle is a shift in perception from the ego's way of interpreting what you see to the Holy Spirit's. It's shifting our perception from believing we're the figure in the dream, to remembering we are the dreamer of the dream. The miracle shows you who the dreamer is. This new perception will inform your words and actions.

When I am working with clients, I am always joined with the Holy Spirit in my mind. Then I know whatever I say will be helpful to them. I don't evaluate what I say or expect specific responses. I let the person's higher mind work with them through me. Again, it's really one mind. The suggestions I give to Person A will be different than Person B and Person C. What's important is the *content* of love in my mind. The *form* of what I say will automatically follow and be reflected into my words. I don't have to worry about it.

The Course clarifies the role of words and language:

> **The value of the atonement** [accepting the truth that there is no sin, no separation in Reality] **does not lie in the manner in which it is expressed. In fact, if it is used truly, it will inevitably be expressed in whatever way is most helpful to the receiver. This means that a miracle, to attain its full efficacy, must be expressed in a language the recipient can understand without fear. This does not necessarily mean that this is the highest level of communication of which he is capable. It does**

> **mean, however, that this is the highest level of communication of which he is capable *now*. The whole aim of the miracle is to raise the level of communication, not to lower it by increasing fear.** [6]

In other words, be with people where they are. My only job is to choose the Holy Spirit or Jesus as my teacher. Using my role as a therapist is just an example. This is how we can all relate to everyone we meet: without judgment. At the beginning of my sessions I remind myself, "The Holy Spirit can take much better care of my clients than I can." Certainly I use my training as a therapist, but *how* it's used is not up to me. I get out of the way and let the information flow through me to my clients.

Remember...choosing your inner teacher comes first. That choice will reflect outward and into your decisions, roles, relationships and interactions.

CHAPTER 6

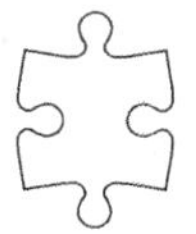

Relationships

Because of guilt, all special relationships have elements of fear in them. This is why they shift and change so frequently.[1]

I'VE NEVER BEEN the kind of person who needed to be in a serious romantic relationship. I enjoy being in them, but I never sought them out. They just seemed to find me and all of a sudden I would think, "Oh, I'm now in a relationship." A theme in a couple of my romantic relationships was co-dependency. I would start out "being myself" and then slowly morph into what I thought my partner wanted me to be. I would lose myself. Because I am naturally laid back and easy going, I would "go with the flow" most of the time. However, once a pattern was established in which I usually did what my partner wanted to do, I would have a hard time voicing my opinion if it were different than his, and when making a decision for myself, I would have trouble standing my ground. My needs and preferences would take a back seat.

I also had the "people pleaser" syndrome! This led to feelings of resentment because I felt like the relationship was unbalanced. All the while, I was the one who didn't stand up for myself. Wow!

When I had been practicing ACIM for a while, I began to understand why this dynamic was playing out. I was able to look at it differently.

Changing the Purpose of Our Relationships so We Can Heal Them

Relationships need to be properly perceived if we are to have any hope of lasting peace and happiness. It's helpful to remember when we're practicing the Course that our "special" relationships in the world are *symbolic* of the one special relationship we have in our mind with our *decision* for the ego thought system. "Special" means separate in the Course; separate from our one true relationship with God. Special relationships are relationships onto which we project our unconscious guilt, substituting them for the real love and true relationship we have with our Creator. All our relationships in the world start off as "special" because they're based on separation from our Source; consequently, they're set up to fail and/or not bring us what we *think* we want!

I have focused on our personal relationships in this book because they give us so much trouble! However, it's important to note that all our relationships here are special, not just our personal ones with people. Any relationship in "the world" is a special relationship because it's based on separation. For example, we have relationships with food, substances, pets, and so forth. The ideas discussed in this chapter can be applied to any relationship.

Often after we've been in a relationship for a while, we gradually realize that things are not like they were in the beginning. We're not in the "honeymoon phase" as they call it. Maybe things are not turning out the way we thought they would. Perhaps we should find a different relationship in order to be happy. This next one will be better, we say. "I've grown and learned from my mistakes." While in one sense this is true and learning from our mistakes can be helpful for sure, going from one relationship to another relationship in the world is not the solution. The solution is switching from choosing the ego to choosing the Holy Spirit, from nightmare dreams of fear to happy dreams of forgiveness. We begin to recognize the choice is really between the "special" relationship and the "Holy" relationship *in the mind*, not between *which* special relationships we have in the world. This is a very important distinction.

Enter the Course's concept of forgiveness. Without forgiveness of our grievances, there will still be problems with any "new" relationship because we're still trying to find peace in relationships by manipulating form — changing our behavior, hoping others will change theirs, or by using any number of external methods in the world.

Now, to be sure, we do want to address bad or unwanted behaviors here and it's helpful to go to counseling if you feel inspired to do so. It's also helpful to have open and honest communication with others. These are things we naturally do. However, if the underlying *purpose* for the relationship is the ego's, then we'll remain in trouble. Why? Because one of the characteristics of the ego thought system (as if sin, guilt and fear weren't bad enough) is lack. The ego is based on scarcity and lack. This shows up in our relationships as needing to get something from another person, situation or object in order to be happy. I often lightly joke with my clients, "You have a relationship with *yourself* your whole life, so why not get that in order first!" In relation to ACIM, that means that we first remember to take responsibility for our projection and even though it's hard, *try to ask the Holy Spirit to help you perceive a relationship through the lens of true forgiveness instead of judgment before making any decisions.* Then whatever is best for everyone will be at the forefront of that choice. Your mind will be at peace about any decision because the *purpose* of your relationship is the Holy Spirit's.

How will you *experience* the choice for the Holy Spirit instead of the ego?

1. You'll be less reactionary.

2. You won't feel offended by comments; you'll interpret your partner's anger as a call for love — they are in fear just like you are when you attack.

3. You'll be able to hear your partner better and respond after truly listening to their point of view.

4. You won't have to be right! You will be stating your preferences or point of view with peace in your mind; there's no need to "convince" anyone of anything.

5. Compromise will be a clear option because you won't interpret what they say as an attack; this will improve discussions and prevent major blow ups!

What I realized in my own life was that I was always giving my power away in relationships — taking a back seat — so people wouldn't be upset if I disagreed with them. I realized I must not have valued myself very much. Not only that, but hidden underneath was the arrogance that it was somehow my fault when people were upset and therefore it was up to me to fix it. How did I attempt this? By trying to manage their feelings by changing my behavior. What!? "This is insane", I realized. Here's how ACIM helped me:

If you're someone who has low self-worth or if you have trouble standing up for yourself, you are buying right into the ego's game! This is one of the ego's tricks to convince you you're a body, and that you're lacking in some way. I started to realize that God in Heaven does not hold an unfavorable opinion of me, but that I had made that up along with the whole world in order to experience myself as separate, unfairly treated, sinful, and not worthy or deserving peace and happiness. As my work progressed with the Course it became a relief that God did not even know of this body — Jackie — whom the ego made up. It was a relief when I remembered that we have a perfect home to wake up to when we heal our belief in separation once and for all!

So what happened was each time I started taking responsibility for someone's anger or discomfort and tried to fix it, I would stop. I said to myself, "This is not my fault and I am not this person's savior. Furthermore, 'I' don't know what's truly helpful in this situation — the Holy Spirit does. This person is not separate from me and I will not intrude my past thinking on them now."

Then I felt better immediately because I was not judging myself or them in that moment. I was able to let go and let the Holy Spirit guide my response. Bye, bye ego interference! The ego cannot survive without judgment. It was my job to look at the relationship differently, with my new teacher.

The Holy Spirit's purpose is to remind you there is no separation in Reality. You are innocent and so are they. This is how you think about another person.

Special relationships take two forms in dreamland:

> **Special hate justifies the projection of guilt by attack; special love conceals the attack within the illusion of love, where we believe our special needs are met by special people with special attributes, for which we love them: in this sense, special love is roughly equivalent to dependency, which breeds contempt or hatred.[2]**

Of course, this is unconscious to us until we start to wake up.

How does the above meaning translate into what we experience daily in our relationships? We know that if people don't meet our perceived needs, then special love becomes special hate rather quickly! Everything in the world is about bargaining. I'll do this for you if you do that for me. We may not even realize this.

You've probably experienced people or situations meeting your needs in one moment and disappointing you in the next. Even those we love will do things that disappoint us or upset us. What happened to our love bargains? There's no consistency because the ego set it up that way. Our salvation will not be found *in* relationships, but in how we *look* at them. After properly perceiving them, they will sometimes change for the better in the world, but it won't always happen and changes in people or the world isn't what the Course is asking you to focus on. We're asked to focus on the content of love in our right mind (cause) and let the relationship we have with another (effect) play out without ego interference.

ACIM teaches that when our relationship in the mind becomes Holy — meaning we've chosen the Holy Spirit instead of the ego — then all our relationships in the world become Holy. Not because people's behavior always changes or because we suddenly all get along, but because the mind's choice for the relationship with the Holy Spirit instead of the ego's special relationships, *is reflected into the projection to bless everyone with the Holy Spirit's perception.* You will *interpret* all your relationships through that lens.

In contrast, relationships seen through the ego's lens focus on service to the personal self and getting our individual needs met, first and foremost. It keeps us focused on what seems to be a myriad of behavior problems in all our different relationships. We're then focused on changing our behavior or wanting others to change theirs so we're happy. This keeps us away from the one true problem of having chosen "specialness" and separation in the mind instead of forgiveness and the miracle. Your practice is to remember this when you get triggered. All our relationships in the world can be given to the Holy Spirit so we can learn our lessons of forgiveness; we learn to go back to the mind that first chose to be separate, and now we make another choice. For example, "I am willing to see this person or situation through the lens of innocence instead of guilt." Since the idea of separation has never left the mind, that means all our relationships are in the mind and therefore we can change our *mind* about them.

ACIM isn't about being a doormat or not addressing behavioral issues in a relationship. It's asking us to first change our mind and lead from the Holy Spirit's thought system. Then you'll intuitively know what's best and your words will flow through the right mind to whomever you're talking to.

For example, when I'm triggered by something my husband says, I stop in that moment before responding. This becomes automatic with practice. I pause and the Holy Spirit takes over my mind. I think of my husband and I as being perfect Spirit and I remember that this is a relationship role that's been scripted out by the ego to experience separation. My husband's comment that triggered me reminds me I've decided for the ego. Simultaneously, I'm also reminded that his comment is not the problem, no matter what it is. I have two ways to interpret his comment. This is challenging at first. But stay with me here.

Since I am watching a projection coming from my own mind, I can either make it real and respond as if I'm offended or attacked, or I can remember this is my projection and let the inner kindness of my right mind guide my response. Even if I strongly disagree with what he said, the energy and temperament of my response is very different when coming from the right mind — it has to be. It won't be reactive. I can still make my point and we often have to agree to disagree, but I have peace as the backdrop in my mind guiding my responses instead of frustration or anger. This is switching to the forgiveness script.

What changes when we listen to our right mind is that we're no longer worried about *what* to say; sometimes what we say in response changes and sometimes it doesn't. But *how* we respond changes. This is the practice of ACIM. This will make a huge difference in your interactions with others.

Another thing that happens in relationships is that you'll say something kind or supportive, but the person takes offense and thinks you meant something different. So even if you are being kind to someone, they might experience it as unkind or think you have an agenda. Why? Because the ego is suspicious and on the lookout for unfair treatment here in the world and, what's more, secretly feels it deserves it. Remember that the ego has *guilt* as its content in the mind and guilt demands punishment. The *content* of the ego thought system is guilt, so it would follow if we're starting from that premise, that this is what we experience. It's truly astonishing to witness this within yourself or notice it in others. It has become painstakingly clear to me when I'm listening to the ego. Jesus says:

> **Beware of the temptation to perceive yourself unfairly treated.**[3]

So, even if you're being kind to someone, the person will sometimes be offended, as if they were being attacked. It is truly remarkable to observe this as it is happening. My job is to be aware of this and not be taken in by appearances.

We will be on a merry-go-round in our relationships and never have permanent *inner* peace about them unless we take the Holy Spirit's hand, which will change their *purpose.* The Holy Spirit's purpose is to see everyone we meet without judgment. This "seeing everyone" means how you're *thinking* about them regardless of behavior you are witnessing. Remember that judgment in the Course is condemnation. When we are ensnared by the ego, we *believe* the differences we see between people (their beliefs, habits and so forth) are real and then we judge those differences.

If I'm triggered and I feel I'm about to attack anyone in thought or word, I recite this quote to myself in my mind as a reminder to lift me out of judgment. I give the situation over to the Holy Spirit to judge for me:

> **Take this from me and look upon it, judging it for me. Let me not see it as a sign of sin and death, nor use it for destruction. Teach me how *not* to make of it an obstacle to peace, but let You use it for me, to facilitate its coming.[4]**

After much practice over the years, I've seemed to shorten it in my mind to "I am willing to use this situation for peace, not as an obstacle to it."

This is my starting point. This shifts my *purpose* for the relationship. I now reflect the Holy Spirit's purpose for it, which is to join, instead of the ego's purpose, which is to separate. Again, joining in ACIM is always about how you're *thinking* about the other person. It's ending the "specialness" of the relationship in my mind; it's ending the reason the ego has given to the relationship, not changing the *form* of the relationship. The form may or may not change. That will play out as it's supposed to. Your job is to get the ego out of the way. With the ego out of the way, you'll have peace *regardless* of the circumstances. ACIM is not talking about joining as bodies — ever. Relationships are the classrooms where we learn to undo the ego thought system in the *mind* — classrooms in which we learn to let go of our guilt.

If you end up physically separating from a person, a job or situation in the world, you would do it peacefully if you have the right teacher in mind. This is often confusing to people when studying the Course. We believe that the Holy Spirit will tell us if we should leave or stay in a certain relationship or job. However, the Holy Spirit is in your *mind* reminding you of your one problem — your *belief* in the ego thought system. He's helping you heal your "special" relationship with the ego. The Holy Spirit would say, "What person? What job?" The truth is that nothing has happened in Reality. The Holy Spirit does not respond to events in a dream; that would make the dream real.

After joining with the Holy Spirit, your right mind can translate that peace into inspiring you to stay or leave a situation. You will have peace about it. Your mind made up the relationship and it has also made up an outcome. This is what the mind does. You can stay or leave angrily or peacefully. Whatever the outcome is, you can be assured you'll be okay and feel peaceful if the Holy Spirit was called upon.

I endeavor to follow inspired guidance all the time. However, if there's any doubt about the guidance, or if it doesn't bring me peace, I remember to ask myself, "Which voice do I want to follow in the dream?" One will bring me peace and the other will reinforce guilt, fear and doubt. This brings me out of focusing on "specific" guidance in the world and back to the mind that reminds me the world is in my mind. Then I'm back at peace and that peace will take *form* in the dream somehow, an inspired idea perhaps, and that is what I follow. As you get used to hearing the Holy Spirit's Voice, you'll withdraw investment in *what* happens in favor of having peace *no matter what happens.*

Your *purpose* is to use every relationship to go back to the mind where you made the first "special" relationship with the *ego* real to yourself. That relationship with the ego is made Holy through true forgiveness and accepting the atonement principle for yourself. Remember the atonement principle says the separation never happened. You're still safe at home with God.

You don't ever have to worry about what to decide. Although you may often receive guidance on specific matters, and that's normal for the mind, it is wise first to ask the Holy Spirit to help you see the person or situation as it truly is — an opportunity to accept the gift your brother has for you — the choice to see him as whole and innocent. Then that is how you see yourself.

Practice *thinking* of him as pure Spirit. You can have comfort knowing the Holy Spirit is with you and what happens will be the best for all concerned.

In the above example with my husband, Mark, I remember that all triggers are my clue to stop and not automatically judge the situation. I remember this was part of my script and that when I ask for help from the Holy Spirit, I am able to let things play out *without ego interference.* This means letting go of the idea that we're separate and that I, as Jackie, know what's best. If there's an "I," then I'm in the ego thought system and will believe I need to correct my situation in the world right away. Further, I will be convinced that I know the best way to go about it. It always involves getting my needs met in some way. When I'm in the right mind I'm at peace, *whatever the outcome.* I'm able to just be and watch things play out in the dream. I know who Mark really is; he is part of the symbolic contents of my own mind, as am I. There is no judgment, only forgiveness.

Whatever you decide to do in your relationships, have your goal be to see them properly first. If you can come from the Holy Spirit's thought system (cause) you'll be in peace not pieces. The outcome (effect) will take care of itself.

"Should I stay or go" becomes "I am willing to see my brother without sin. I forgive my projected images of this person and myself for dreaming them." Then let it go. The Holy Spirit retranslates the purpose of the relationship and uses it as a classroom for forgiveness.

Now you're at cause (the mind) and not at effect (the world). Your final decision will come naturally as you play out the "forgiveness" script instead of the "ego's" script.

When it comes to abuse of any kind it's important to protect yourself. There are many people in abusive relationships. Leaving is an obvious choice if you're in physical danger. There's nothing "spiritual" about staying in an abusive relationship because you're "learning lessons." That is not being kind to yourself. It's also letting someone continue behavior that's in no one's best interest. You can ask the Holy Spirit to be with you when you remember to think of it. This way of thinking can be with you in your mind, as you're doing what's best and taking steps to keep yourself safe.

In summary, since we project our guilt outside of the mind onto our relationships in the world, that's where our work is. That's where we begin — where we believe we are — and indeed where our current experience is. So our relationships serve the purpose of looking at the distress and pain we're experiencing with our new internal teacher. This is what the Workbook of the Course helps us do: go from mindlessness — identifying with the personal, individual self — to returning to the mind and viewing the body in action from an observer standpoint.

The miracle is shifting our focus from the body to the mind. The miracle shows you who the dreamer is. Then from that place, as the observer of the ego in action from above the battleground (decision-making part of the mind), we can contrast the two dreams; the ego's dream of separation and the Holy Spirit's dream of forgiveness. When we're caught up "in the dream" as the body we're identifying with, it's hard to remember that we made this up and that the "cause" of the world we see is because of a decision our mind made.

This is why the Course teaches there is only one special relationship — our relationship with the ego thought system. That thought of sin guilt and fear gets projected out of the mind and takes the form of all our relationships in the world. But this is a projection. We do start with the projection, but only to recognize our distress so we will be motivated to go back to the mind, and to change our mind to the Holy Spirit's script. The Holy Spirit's script is still part of the illusion, however, we need to move in the right direction and change our nightmare dreams into happy dreams before we awaken. Peace is the condition of the Kingdom of Heaven, so we can't enter with a conflicted mind. One goal of the Course is inner peace.

A Tranquil mind is not a little gift.[5]

When we choose the Holy Spirit as our teacher, in that Holy Instant all our relationships become Holy because that is what the mind *reflects* outward. It doesn't continue to project guilt into the dream world; rather, it extends forgiveness. You will *experience* all your relationships differently!

Holy relationships are not between bodies. Bodies are just the projection. The Holy relationship is in the mind. It is between you and Jesus or the Holy Spirit when you choose them as your teacher.

Yes, we still work on our relationships here, but we want to remember to take the ego out of the way. All the ego does is bargain. Let's go for inner peace and joy instead!

Nugget of Wisdom

Here's how I practice: Whatever I have to forgive, meaning whatever upsets me during the day or whatever I'm judging, that's what I use as my classroom. I bring the stressors of everyday life to the quiet center within me. I bring my concerns, things I wish were different, things I'm resisting, whatever it is. I bring it to Jesus to look at it with me. Gradually your experience will shift from the ego being front and center to the right mind being front and center. You will notice this difference because you won't be as reactionary; things won't bother you as much. You will be able to remember more easily that you're dreaming. You will begin to shift *how* you look at everything! You have to because you're leading from a different part of your mind. This is a gradual process for most people, because as the ego loses its grip on you, it becomes very threatened. It will fight for its existence! But you can turn the tables on it. You turn the tables on the ego by looking at its antics without judgment or condemnation, not by fighting against it. "Fighting" anything makes it real to your mind.

When you're making these shifts, your outer world won't always change in *form*. That's okay. Just honor where you and where others are on your respective paths. Be gentle with yourself and others. Be kind. All will be well.

CHAPTER 7

Who Is the Holy Spirit and How Does He Help Us?

> **The Holy Spirit's function is to take the broken picture of the Son of God and put the pieces into place again. This holy picture, healed entirely, does He hold out to every separate piece that thinks it is a picture in itself.[1]**

THE HOLY SPIRIT is described in the Course as God's answer to the belief in separation. The Course is teaching that we seemingly separated from our perfect Oneness, our perfect Unity in Heaven. The Holy Spirit, therefore, is a communication link between God and His separated Sons. He is the memory that we took into this dream with us, so He sees our illusions without believing in them. He reminds us of our shared interest in going home. He also employs our shared purpose of forgiveness to reunite the broken pieces of our fragmented dream of separation. He is also called the Voice for God, who speaks for Him, and for our real Self, reminding us of the identity that we forgot. In short, the Holy Spirit helps us by reminding us, "nothing has happened, you're still at home with your Creator." We remember this by healing one piece of the dream at a time.

The Holy Spirit is also referred to as the Bridge. Why do we need a Bridge? Because we still believe we are separate from our Source, that there is a gap. The Holy Spirit's Voice is a reminder that there is no gap. The Course is a purely non-dualistic teaching, meaning that 'God Is.' In other words, the realm of Heaven is, and nothing else is. There's a wonderful section in the text called "The Quiet Answer." In this section Jesus tells us that all of our forms of questioning, when we're asking for help with externals, are a form of propaganda for the ego. Meaning, their purpose is to keep us believing that our bodies, everyone else's bodies and the whole physical universe — the whole time-space dream — is real.

> **Thus is all questioning within the world a form of propaganda for itself.**[2]

Asking for help takes many forms: Help finding the right life partner, finding the right job, help with paying our monthly bills, help with making the right decision, or help in healing from an illness.

The ego keeps its game going when we ask the Holy Spirit to fix something for us externally. If we do this, we're making the world real, thus keeping us mindless in a world we believe is our real home. Rather, we are asked to give over the seeming problem, in whatever form it takes, to the Holy Spirit for the best outcome for all concerned. The true answer that *A Course in Miracles* teaches is the quiet answer; the recognition that all our *seeming* problems stem from one problem — the belief in our separation from our Source. All our problems in the world are symbolic of our choice for separation in the mind.

> **In quietness are all things answered, and is every problem quietly resolved.**[3]

Every problem is quietly resolved because there is no hierarchy of illusions. An illusion is an illusion is an illusion. They are all resolved in the same way because they are all untrue.

The Course reminds us that we're making the error of separation real by continuously asking for help *in* the world. I'd like to paraphrase an interesting example of the answer that Jesus gave to Helen Schucman, scribe of the Course, when she asked what she should say to someone who needed help. Keep in mind she was asking for "specific" help. Jesus told Helen not to ask Him what she should say to her brother. Ask Him instead to help her see her brother through the eyes of truth and not judgment. Ken Wapnick commented on this, saying Jesus' message to Helen was to ask Him rather to remove the judgment in her mind so she would intuitively know the most loving response.

ACIM is teaching us to ask for help in removing the blocks to the awareness of love's presence, so we can eventually hear only one voice. Then we will know intuitively what to say and do. This Voice for God (Holy Spirit) is not *in* the dream at all — that Voice is outside of time and space, not talking to us as an individual, not to me as Jackie, but to the decision-making mind, the one mind that believes it's here and has taken on a separate identity.

The Holy Spirit or Jesus' answers are reminding us *in our mind* what we are in truth. They remind us we forgot to laugh at this tiny, mad idea of separation in the beginning, when we had a choice between wholeness and a separate identity.

So, to give you an example of my own practice, I always start off the day by putting the Holy Spirit in charge. It's automatic now because I've been practicing these principles for many years. I automatically wake up and know the Holy Spirit is in charge of my day. I don't always have to physically say it, although I often do, because it is a good reminder and sets a good tone for the day.

This puts me in a miracle-ready position. During the day whenever I get upset or confused, whenever I question what I should do, I am reminded I don't need to decide anything in that moment with the ego as my teacher. If I feel upset in any way, I say, "Oh, that's right! The ego must be in charge because I'm confused, indecisive or not at peace. If I choose to listen, the Holy Spirit will retranslate this *seeming* problem and confusion in the world for me." I think to myself, "Let me step back for a moment and remember my real problem — my belief that I'm separate from God. I was believing that I was alone in the world and had to figure something out on my own or look for help outside myself."

People in the world will always have conflicting opinions. Sometimes their opinions will be helpful and sometimes not — they'll further confuse you — all to the ego's delight!

The point is that when I remember the above statements in my mind, it puts me in a relaxed state. I remember that "I," Jackie, don't need to figure this out in this moment. This thought to see my situation another way comes quickly because the Holy Spirit is in charge of my day. When I get confused or frustrated, my right mind immediately reinterprets my purpose. I chose the Holy Spirit's perspective at the beginning of the day, so everything that happens is used for His purpose instead of the ego's. This is the power of your mind! I'm already in a miracle state-of-readiness in the morning. I am miracle-ready instead of judgment-ready. It changes the entire experience of my day, not necessarily what happens in my day.

Which Teacher Will You Listen To?

I love this quote from Sitting Bull, a Native American Chief: "Inside of me there are two dogs. One is mean and evil and the other is good and they fight each other all the time. When asked which one wins I answer, the one I feed the most."

Because your experience follows your thought, whichever part of the mind you're listening to, that is what you're going to experience out in the world. So, if you're listening to the ego, you're going to experience pain and suffering caused by a myriad of problems that you believe are outside of you and very real. Your identity is threatened. You have to solve things immediately or there will be dire consequences. You might think, "Oh my gosh, I don't know how I'm going to pay these extra bills." Fear of not having enough money engulfs you. You panic and feel desperate to come up with an answer.

However, when you're listening to the Holy Spirit, your mind will reinterpret the situation as a lesson, a means to learn through the power of true forgiveness, to experience inner peace no matter what. You are learning how to better handle any issue with the right teacher. For example, after feeling the initial fear at the appearance of two new bills to pay, you would remember to stop in that moment. Listening to the Holy Spirit I say to myself, "Oh, I just received two new hospital bills in the mail; this is another opportunity. I'm upset about this. I'm afraid. Please look at this with me. I must have pushed away love today. But I'm not upset for the reason I think. I'm afraid because I've made the situation real in my mind; I must have been listening to the ego as my teacher. Nothing has happened in Reality and I will trust the Holy Spirit in this moment."

This doesn't mean you don't want answers to your problems and doesn't mean you don't have an immediate situation that needs to be addressed. But, we can research solutions on the Internet in a state of frenzy or a state of calm. We can call and ask people for help in a state of panic or we can call and say, "You know, I was wondering if you might have some insight on this." It's all a matter of your starting point. Noticing your upset reaction and looking at it with the Holy Spirit, thus changing your starting point, makes all the difference.

So, our situations have been scripted out here in the world. This means that in the instant the seeming separation thought occurred, every dream and every possible ego choice occurred and was instantaneously corrected by the Holy Spirit. All events are fixed in this sense. But our *experience* of our circumstances can be different depending on which thought system is active in our mind in any given moment. And what the Course is helping us do is be active to the Holy Spirit and passive to the ego. All the Holy Spirit does, much to the ego's upset, is remind us gently — "Remember, you are safe at home. Nothing has happened." This is how we slowly start to undo the belief in the false self so the real Self will eventually be all that's left.

Forgiveness is still. It waits, it *does* nothing. What does it wait for? For you to change your mind. By not reacting to the world as real in your mind, it *undoes* the separation. It recalls your projection because you're not giving the illusion the kind of fearful attention the ego would have you give it. From a calmer state, from an awareness that you're not alone, you're able to look at everything differently and proceed from that point. Your right mind will retranslate your situation automatically. The right-minded thought system will then inform all your words and actions. You won't even have to worry about it.

Here is a question from the Foundation for *A Course in Miracles* website which illustrates this point further. The person asks:

"I've been studying ACIM since 1977 and although I understand the theory, I unfortunately cannot translate the theory into my life situation."

We can all relate to this statement. Sometimes it's hard to practically apply the Course teachings because we forget that the Course is only about mind and how you're thinking. It has nothing to do with behavior. And that is understandably a stumbling block for a lot of people. The questioner goes on to say, "By a series of circumstances, I am at the point of ruin and bankruptcy. I read the lesson that tells me to step back, and let the spirit lead the way. How do you do that? How do you know that it is spirit? I try to let it lead. Yet, I must be doing something wrong because here I stand at the edge."

I think we can all relate to this person's experience because sometimes we have circumstances staring us in the face and we are desperate. We lose a job, we're having struggles in a relationship, a parent or child gets sick, a loved one passes away, you are diagnosed with an illness — whatever it is. These are things that are very hard and very difficult to deal with. So, the Course is always about being normal and doing the normal thing. What the Course would say is, "Which teacher do you choose to experience this with?" This is not ever about denying problems or not looking at a situation. It is about recognizing that you can look at your situation through either one of two lenses. Which thought are you going to have in your mind, first, before you proceed with anything that you do?

Here is the answer from Ken Wapnick and the Foundation for *A Course in Miracles* (FACIM):

> We easily fall into the trap of believing that the Holy Spirit's answer to our call for help would be a change in the external situation — the world or the body. We forget that problems in our bodies and the world are the *effect*, and the *cause* is our belief that we separated from God and destroyed love to achieve that separation. Thus in Chapter 27, Jesus reminds us that the Holy Spirit
>
> "Looks not to effects...He bids you bring each terrible effect to Him that you may look together on its foolish cause and laugh with Him a while. *You* judge effects, but *He* has judged their cause. And by His judgment are effects removed. Perhaps you come in tears. But hear him say, 'My brother, holy Son of God, behold your idle dream, in which this could occur.' And you will leave the holy instant with your laughter and your brother's joined with His."

Then it goes on to say:

> Understandably, this may not be very consoling when you are on the verge of ruin, and you would much prefer that the Holy Spirit intervene to make things better for you in the world. He can't, because He doesn't see a world. He would help you get to the point where you share that perception with Him, so that you would be at peace regardless of what seems to be happening outside you. The problem is we don't realize — and probably don't believe — that what Jesus and the Holy Spirit say is outside us is really outside us.

We think that our identity is really us in the world, but the Holy Spirit knows that it is not. The quote continues:

> How better could He help us, then, than to teach us how to begin the process of dis-identifying with our identities as part of the world; and what better time to do that than when we are deeply troubled by problems in the world and our bodies. Challenging, yes; and seemingly impossible, yes. But this is what the Course is about. And that does not mean that you should not do everything you possibly can to rectify the financial situation — consulting a financial advisor, etc.
>
> Jesus assures us many times that if we walk our path with the willingness to grow to value nothing but his love, and to accept that as our real identity, we can go through the most horrendous (from the world's point of view) situations and still be at peace within. That is not easy, and it means letting go of any investment in having the problem in the world be solved in a particular way.[4]

Alright, so let's take that in for a moment. It's a very deep teaching in the sense that — let's be honest — it goes against everything that we believe and that we want to hear when we're in a crisis. And to be sure, we do start out always by asking for specific help in the world; indeed, it's what we've been taught and encouraged by the ego to do. All over the world people are taught to pray for specific outcomes to specific problems. This is okay. Sometimes we get them. However, the Course is teaching that eventually we want to move up the rungs of the spiritual ladder, so to speak, and broaden our understanding of what true prayer is. The "Song of Prayer" supplement, an accompaniment to the Course, discusses our journey in going from praying for specifics to eventually asking for nothing and joining with God knowing we have everything. We bask in the love of knowing we are well taken care of. True prayer — as taught by the Course — is a high bar. It will be addressed more in-depth in a future book.

If you remember this is your dream, just like you remember a dream that you had in bed last night that cannot possibly affect you, you will be able to address your crisis or problem from your new starting point, which is the right mind where the Holy Spirit resides. Like Dorothy, we've all had dreams in bed at night that seem very real, and yet when we wake up, they're gone. Where are they? They've disappeared. Why? Because they were never really there. Why? Because the mind made them up!

So the Course is teaching us that all of our time is spent in dreaming. When we leave our nocturnal dreams and seemingly wake up in the morning, we're waking up to another form of dreaming. This is why the Course is only about mind. It teaches that mind is all there is. It's teaching that the world is *in* the mind. The world is a projection of the mind, the mind which is outside of time and space.

When you really understand and integrate what the Course is teaching about the mind and body, it will change everything for you. Is it unsettling at first? Of course! It'll be unsettling along the journey because we'll keep saying "But what about this...! But what about that?!' Eventually it brings more comfort than strife because siding with the Holy Spirit puts you back in your true power — at cause, with the power to choose once again followed by the accompanying feeling of peace. You know that you, as mind, can choose to see the world differently. Jesus specifically addresses our skepticism, the uncertainties we have with these ideas and the reluctance to embrace them. In the "Introduction" to the Workbook, He says:

> **Some of the ideas the workbook presents you will find hard to believe, and others may seem to be quite startling. This does not matter. You are merely asked to apply the ideas as you are directed to do. You are not asked to judge them at all. You are asked only to use them. It is their use that will give them meaning for you, and will show you that they are true.[5]**

Let's revisit the popular line mentioned earlier:

> **Seek not to change the world, but choose to change your *mind* about the world.**[6]

That's not a small distinction. It's challenging at first, but what happens over time is that the more we make the choice for the Holy Spirit, the easier it becomes to integrate the Course's concepts when you're confronted with problems of any kind. An illusion is an illusion is an illusion. All problems are looked at and forgiven in the same way. This heals your unconscious guilt which eliminates the need to continue projecting it outside yourself.

The Holy Spirit starts taking over your mind and you start to favor spiritual Vision over your physical sight. The Course understands that you need to settle your problems in the world. This is what we would normally do. However, it teaches us to change our internal teacher first, when we remember to do it. If you do this you'll have a very different experience of your life, no matter what is happening around you. You are the cause of the dream and you can change your mind about its purpose. You can choose to believe in illusions and keep dreaming, or you can take responsibility for your projection, forgive your projected images and yourself for projecting them, and wake up. Trust the Holy Spirit. What to "do" will come intuitively as a reflection of that choice.

So the next time you are looking at other figures in the dream that are *seemingly* the cause of your problem, or if you are seemingly causing problems for others, you can remember to stop in that moment and forgive. Choose the miracle. Jesus is teaching that true forgiveness is actually forgiving your brother for what he hasn't done. Not because you're more advanced spiritually, not because you're on a spiritual path and the other person is not, not because you're taking the high road, not because they don't know what they're doing, but because *what you're seeing is not true.*

How can events happening in a dream be true? We're asked to forgive all the differences the body's eyes are showing us. The body's eyes were made by the ego to see form and judge the differences. With the Course's form of forgiveness, we're not forgiving behaviors, but something more fundamental. We are forgiving ourselves for *believing* anyone is really doing anything in an illusory world. We're asked to forgive ourselves for dreaming that we're separate in the first place. Then we can let go and let the Holy Spirit show us that letting go is how we can be in peace. We will still do what's best in the world, but since we've changed our internal teacher, we will proceed with solutions from that awareness. We don't have to worry further.

The Course is teaching there's just one mind that thinks it's here. We acknowledge this truth when we make the choice for the Holy Spirit by thinking or saying something like, "I'm just willing to see this differently. I'm willing NOT to judge my brother and be taken in by appearances. I'm willing to take responsibility for my dream." We say, "I want to be truly helpful. I want to make the world better. I don't want to see suffering." Well, guess what? The Course is teaching that all pain and suffering is a mental process. Truly helping others is going back to our mind and changing our own misperceptions. This re*minds* other minds they can make the same choice when they're ready. Healing is in the mind. It's how we *look* at everything, meaning, which interpretation of the dream will I choose?

When we choose the ego, we reinforce the separation and believe people's bodies are who they really are. The body is the hero of the dream. There's no dream without the body, because the ego made the body as its crowning glory. It says, "See? You exist! You're a body in the world, and look, all your senses witness to the reality of the dream!" Look at how our senses bring back data for the brain to analyze. All the while Jesus is reminding us that the body is the false "you" that came from a false idea that you could be separate from God in any way.

As the Holy Spirit starts taking over your mind, you're looking at people and *thinking* silently, "Oh, they are behaving badly. But that is a call for love. I can remember what is behind that behavior — fear." If they weren't a dreaming mind, believing that they were here, they wouldn't be fearful. Everybody here is fearful. And this is why Jesus wants to help us see beyond the shadow; beyond the projection. He wants us to see our shared interest. We all have the shared interest of going home to Heaven; we just forgot. Everybody's walking around asleep. We share the ego, we share the Holy Spirit, and we share the power to choose between them. Let's choose peace instead of pieces.

Incidentally, it is truly caring to *think* of others as they really are. You will be guided as to what to do on the level of form, meaning with your body in the world. The difference is that the right mind will be informing your functioning and not the ego. You will say exactly what you need to say to people. You will do what's best. If you're in danger of physical attack — run. Do the normal thing. Forgive later when you have more time.

Jesus assures us the practice of true forgiveness gets easier if we are willing to look at things with Him. This is how the Holy Spirit helps us. When do we do it? When we're anything but peaceful. We'll do it if we're motivated. When are we motivated? When something's not going our way and we wish things were different.

Inspired Guidance

Sometimes we notice that we seem to get "inspired guidance." Putting the Holy Spirit in charge of our day facilitates an experience of peace in the mind. The Holy Spirit doesn't give any guidance in a world that isn't there, however, inspiration can be reflected into the dream that takes the form of a helpful idea or symbol when the mind is less conflicted. With less conflict in the mind you aren't suffering as much. You're not suffering as much because your unconscious guilt is being healed and you're punishing yourself less.

I often will be doing something unrelated to a problem I want solved and suddenly, as I'm in the kitchen making dinner, I get an insight on what to do about a particular issue. I know what the real problem is, so as a result of putting the Holy Spirit in charge at the beginning of my day, I didn't spend the day mulling over my "specific" problem with the ego in charge. Because the ego wasn't in charge of my mind, I was not making the problem real, over analyzing it and having to solve it immediately and in a particular way. My *experience* of the day is so different! What if you were able to just let things go when you're confused or distressed and think to yourself, "I can look at this differently if I am willing. I trust that things will play out better if I get the ego out of the way. Our scripts are written here. What do I really have control over in this moment? I have control over my *experience* of these events in this moment."

That's what changes when we hear the Holy Spirit — we take responsibility for our lives. We still have our forgiveness opportunities scripted out for us, but we are aware we have a choice: we can experience things that happen to us peacefully, or feel like we're in pieces. We can be inspired with an idea or two along the way often saving ourselves from needless suffering and worry. These inspired ideas can be seen as a *reflection* of choosing our right-minded teacher.

In conclusion, whenever you are having trouble and looking for a specific answer, remember to let go and know you are doing the best you can in the moment. Tell yourself you're not going to make it worse by judging the problem or yourself for not being able to solve it. The reason why we're confronted with endless problems and why we repeat destructive behaviors is because we're secretly attracted to guilt, and therefore keep doing the things that leave us feeling guilty or frustrated. Remember that it's okay to ask for specifics as you're learning about the healing power of the mind. The mind can accept certain "magic" remedies without fear. At the end of the day, remember that the cause of the problem is the belief in separation. Once the guilt behind a specific problem has been uncovered, released and healed, you'll no longer need to project it outside your mind. Keep practicing!

CHAPTER 8

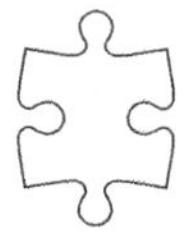

The Keys to Living in This World

> It's quite simple to be happy, but difficult to be simple. — Robert Jackson

A *Course in Miracles* is over 1200 pages long because the ego is complicated. The truth is simple. We have only one problem for which there is one solution.

The reason why this is difficult to accept is because we are so attached to our individual specialness. Not to mention the ego tells us that in order to accomplish anything truly worthwhile, we'll have to go through some blood, sweat and tears. But what if you were patient and pursued your interests without guilt in the mind, without the ego as your teacher? You can move through life without experiencing suffering. It helps me to remember that I'm responding to the way I set things up on another level. I can turn the tables on the ego by seeing the problem as it really is instead of the way I set it up.

> **Now you are being shown you *can* escape. All that is needed is you look upon the problem as it is, and not the way you have set it up. How could there be another way to solve a problem that is very simple, but has been obscured by heavy clouds of complication, which were made to keep the problem unresolved?[1]**

The "heavy clouds of complication" is the guilt we feel that has kept us from recognizing our one and only problem. The only problem is the mind's *belief* in sin which justifies punishment. The mind's *belief* in sin — one of the "secret sins and hidden hates" — gets projected out into the world's dream so it appears that the problem is not our choice for the ego, but rather out there in "the world." Through vigilant practice it's possible to live simply and guilt-free if we are willing to let go and trust the Holy Spirit.

Living simply with the Holy Spirit as my guide is one of the key ingredients for peace of mind!

Below are some other ingredients in my recipe for inner peace. Practicing these principles will get easier and easier, leading to awakening from the dream of time and space that is our life here. The benefits are beyond measure!

Being the Observer

Be aware of your thoughts throughout the day. When we are suffering in any way we are listening to the ego, the false self, and experiencing separation from our Source. The mind's decision for guilt (ego) is the cause of all pain and suffering, both physical and psychological. Remember, we felt guilty seemingly long ago when we threw God's love away in favor of a separate and autonomous self. The pain and suffering scenarios we experience are all symbolic representations of believing in the "tiny mad idea" of separation in the mind.

We can make a different decision — to listen to the Holy Spirit. Remember that you are the observer of the dream. Yes, we are having the *experience* that we are the figure in the dream, but we can be led beyond that experience. You will still be having your normal life here, you'll just be looking at things differently — this is how we start. For example, I can watch myself and observe, "Okay, here is Jackie going to the grocery store; here is Jackie chatting with a neighbor." The habit of noticing your thoughts and what the body is doing are important steps. We watch the ego in action. Who is the one that is watching? The one that is observing is not you as a body. It is you as the decision-making mind, outside of time and space.

When We Get Triggered

So what do we do when something upsets us? Once we are in the habit of observing our daily activities, as in the example above, we can now say to ourselves, "Okay, here's Jackie feeling upset." Or, "I just had a very bad thought about my spouse." Just notice that something has upset you in thought or feeling. You were fine the moment before. Next, look at why you're upset. For example, "I'm so mad that my spouse said this to me!" Whatever you react to is your red flag. Any disruption of peace is not the peace of God, so you must be listening to the wrong-minded teacher. This is your clue to change your internal teacher and *look at the upset with your new teacher.* When you look with the Holy Spirit, your mind will retranslate the upset in a way that will be helpful to you and that can be seen through the right-minded interpretation.

For example, let's say this is your trigger: "My spouse hurt my feelings when my point of view was shut down and I felt small and insignificant. I made a suggestion about our travel schedule and got blasted for my idea!"

There are two interpretations of this:

Ego thinks: I am offended and I have to "attack" back and defend myself. "How could you do this to me over and over? Next time I won't even say anything so there's no conflict. I'm tired of this same old thing!"

Holy Spirit translation: I stop before responding because I recognize this opportunity as a red flag. I am willing to look at this through the lens of peace and not judgment. My spouse is in fear too or else there would not have been an unkind comment or shut down of any kind. My spouse is showing me the content of my own mind (the content is the guilt I feel from separating from God). I forgive my spouse because I recognize that this is my dream and no one can take the peace of God from me except *me.* I forgive my spouse for what he or she hasn't done because this is my projection. He or she is blessing me with an opportunity to choose a miracle instead of a grievance. I also forgive myself for dreaming this dream of separation in the first place. Now I can join with the Holy Spirit in Peace. *These are examples of what the Holy Spirit can remind you of when you are in the moment of upset.* Your right mind will give you ideas that are helpful. This will change *how* you respond.

Example of an ego response: (happens in thought too; they aren't always spoken) "I can't believe you said that! You don't even know what you're saying. That's not even what I mean. I can't tell you my ideas about this anymore." Or "You never listen to me, we always have to do things your way."

This makes the dream real to you. You are in your ego mind because you think your spouse is the cause of your upset. What is really happening is you are being shown the content of your own mind (separation) projected outside yourself. It appears that people are the cause of your up-

set, but in actuality, you put them there when you chose the ego so you could see your own guilt outside of yourself instead of inside your conflicted mind. You are responding to your own projection.

Holy Spirit-inspired response: (with a gentle internal smile, knowing you are not separate) "Maybe I didn't explain my reasoning clearly. I'd like to talk about it for a minute and tell you my side. What is your reasoning for wanting to take an earlier flight?"

You won't have to be concerned with *what* you say when you're thinking with the Holy Spirit. *How* you say whatever you say will be coming from your new teacher. You will intuitively know the best response to the situation. The new interpretation in your mind will guide your words. You are joined with Jesus "above the battleground."

Let's review what Jesus means by going "above the battleground." The battleground is still illusory and it begins with the illusory battle in the wrong mind, which is the seeming conflict between ourselves and God. This conflict gets projected out into the myriad of relationships in the battleground of the world. There is conflict in all relationships.

A Course in Miracles is teaching us that no matter what people do to you, no matter what you do to them or what you merely witness other people doing to each other, it would have no effect on you unless you believe the dream is reality. The purpose of going "above the battle ground" is that the Holy Spirit will retranslate how you see the situation; the mind interprets the data your eyes show you either through the ego's lens or the Holy Spirit's. You will remember that people are either expressing love or calling out for it.

Ken Wapnick clarifies the Course's message that we are not responsible for *what* our eyes report back to us, but rather *how* we interpret what our eyes see. We are responsible for interpreting the symbols and images our eyes see. This is a different way of "seeing." We see through the eyes of Christ which is an attitude of forgiveness. This is how we correct the ego's misperceptions. Remember that eyes were made as part of the illusory body to experience separation so we believe it's real, and to judge the differences in form. The way we are in control of our life is having the power to choose how we *interpret* the world. This determines what our *experience* will be. The right-minded interpretation through the lens of forgiveness is the happy dream that precedes awakening.

Nothing external can affect you because there is nothing external. The world is in the mind. It is a projection of the *thought* of separation in the mind, so the world has never left its source. Let's remember to go to the source!

Joining Him above the battleground means going back to the decision-making mind and looking with Him at our perceived problems and situations that the ego has scripted out for us.

> **The secret of salvation is but this: that you are doing this unto yourself. No matter what the form of attack, this is still true. Whoever**

> **takes the role of enemy and of attacker, still this is the truth. Whatever seems to be the cause of any pain and suffering you feel, this is still true. For you would not react at all to figures in a dream you knew that you were dreaming. Let them be as hateful and vicious as they may, they could have no effect on you unless you failed to recognize it is your dream.**[2]

So, remember to watch your thoughts as you go through your day. The body may appear to be busy on some days and laid back on other days. The quiet center in your mind is the same. Be the observer. Watch your triggers. You'll have lots of practice. We are never deprived of forgiveness opportunities!

Learn to Generalize

There are a multitude of things throughout the day that make us uncomfortable or downright upset. Some we might categorize as minor: someone has more than 12 items in the grocery express line, getting an automated response system instead of an actual customer service person, or being overwhelmed watching fear-based news propaganda. Some we categorize as major — (often personal) such as being diagnosed with a serious illness or losing a job which is your livelihood.

But Jesus is asking us to recognize that the *cause* of any upsets or disturbances of our peace are the same regardless of the *form* they take in the world. There is no hierarchy of illusions. An illusion is an illusion is an illusion. He's also teaching us that a mild annoyance is no different that intense anger, fury or rage because *none* of these states are the peace of God. Fortunately:

> **There is no order of difficulty in miracles. One is not "harder" or "bigger" than another. They are all the same. All expressions of love are maximal.**[3]

One miracle is not harder to perform than another. Illusions of any kind can be forgiven in the same way *because* they are all untrue. Everything in the projection we call "the world" is forgiven in the same way because all of it is made up. The fact that we think some things are more serious than others (which indeed they are in the dream and we address each situation in the best way we can), is an ego trick to keep us focused on the world instead of the mind that made it.

This does not mean that we are experiencing everything as the same. Certainly, having a serious illness is different than having to wait in an annoying line. The Course merely asks us to begin noticing how we are *thinking* about these different people, situations and events, and how quickly we give our peace away. What *is* the same is that they are all part of the same illusion and are all untrue. This is the template we hold in our minds. There's always something in the world to upset you and take away the peace in your mind, whatever the form.

This attitude is key. No matter what goes on in your life, you have the power of decision in your mind. You can decide for peace or not. It doesn't mean that you won't have a bad situation happen, but your *experience* of that situation is dependent on your internal teacher. If you start your day with the goal of inner peace, then everything that comes up for you during the day will be used for that purpose. This is how you can be miracle-ready instead of judgment-ready. When the trigger happens, your right mind will use the situation as your forgiveness classroom with your goal being inner peace instead of conflict. This is powerful and can direct your functioning throughout the day. You won't be as reactionary as you would be with the ego as your teacher. This will improve the *experience* of your life in so many ways!

We are generalizing interpretations in the mind not generalizing from form to form. In our behavior, we will deal with a serious illness differently than with a stubbed toe. We will exercise common sense and take the necessary steps to take care of ourselves as best we can. The sameness in these scenarios is what we are *thinking*; what our attitude is toward each problem. This is what wakes us up! Believing in the mind's illusions keeps them in place. However, since we believe in them we are taught how to let them go slowly. Forgiveness is the process.

We all have difficult times. So, who do you want to go through them with? How has listening to the ego worked out for you up to this point? What do you have to lose if you invite the Holy Spirit to look at your issues with you? Your issues may not disappear right away, but your *experience* of them will change. It's worth it! The choice for the Holy Spirit will be comforting, helping you remember:

I could see peace instead of this.[4]

Beyond Positive Thinking

> Positive thinking will only get you so far when you're positively thinking there's a world outside of you. — Jackie Lora Jones

Why do most New Age approaches only get you so far? Because they are always looking for answers in an illusion from *within* the illusion!

All my life people have called me a positive person and I always appreciate their kind words. However, while I know looking on the bright side of things is certainly helpful, I've learned that just changing a negative thought to a positive one *is not forgiving it.*

What are we trying to achieve by thinking positively? We want to feel better or create a better experience for ourselves. We want to make the dream better. We're often encouraged to see the glass as half full. What happens, though, is that nothing will permanently change because we're making the world real to our mind by just focusing on externals getting better. Thinking positively will not undo our guilt that stems from our hidden belief that we've sinned and are separate from each other and from God.

The Course is not a course in love and positive thinking. It's a course in uncovering and undoing the negative, so the real you is all that's left:

The Course does not aim at teaching the meaning of love, for that is beyond what can be taught. It does aim, however, at removing the blocks to the awareness of love's presence, which is your natural inheritance.[5]

Thinking positively does not undo the ego. Indeed, it's helpful to think positively because we temporarily feel better. I look on the bright side all the time. However, the Course gently reminds me that what I really want is something permanent; an inner peace I can always have no matter what is happening to me or around me.

The Course is teaching that if we want a permanent change in how we feel and want to undo the false self, it's necessary to go beyond just thinking positively. The key is to look at our negative thoughts without judgment or fear. This is what it means to look with your right mind. One thing that helps me practice is to remember: The negative or unwanted thoughts I have are not "me." I don't have to be afraid to look at them. I just have to be willing to forgive them. We all have good and bad thoughts all the time. It's built into the ego thought system of duality. Whether you happen to be thinking good thoughts or bad thoughts, it's not "you." The fact that you are thinking at all is evidence that you are in a separated state of illusion. In Heaven there is no thinking. There's an awareness of perfect oneness.

We are asked to bring our negative thoughts to the light of truth. Looking at our dark thoughts with our right-minded teacher dispels them. Otherwise the thoughts stay buried and we never undo the guilt that's behind them. Looking without judgment (observing) is how we transform our thinking and shift our experience from nightmares to happy dreams. Forgiveness and the miracle are the means we use to transform our thinking:

> **The miracle establishes you dream a dream, and that its content is not true. This is a crucial step in dealing with illusions. No one is afraid of them when he perceives he made them up. The fear was held in place because he did not see that he was the author of the dream, and not the figure in the dream.**[6]

Sometimes we don't have the motivation to let our attack thoughts go because it's a part of who we *believe* we are. Who would we be without our grievances? Who would we be without our problems?

It's true that we didn't choose our life circumstances on this level, meaning the world, where we believe we are. When our mind chose the idea of fragmentation over wholeness at the beginning of our dream, all our seeming lifetimes were made in that instant. If we want to truly heal and heal permanently, we can recognize our mistaken choice for separation long ago and choose again *now*. When do we choose? When there's something to forgive, or when we feel anything less than peaceful and wish things were different. We are never deprived of forgiveness opportunities!

No one would argue that it is not helpful to reach for a higher thought when you feel bad. Many New Age teachings tell us to be in a higher vibration. There's nothing wrong with that. It's a normal thing we do. However, ACIM reminds us that it is in bringing our dark thoughts to the light of truth that we heal our minds. This means *looking* at them with the Holy Spirit as our teacher whenever and wherever they arise. Changing negative thoughts to positive thoughts or living in a higher vibration, while temporarily helpful, is still making the world real by believing that positive thoughts or higher vibrational living will bring us what we want. These approaches are still rooted in a separation idea. We ultimately want to be free of *all illusions* so there's no need for anything. Seeking answers in the illusion from within the illusion will help us feel better temporarily, and as I said, I've used several of these approaches through the years. What I've learned is that they won't undo the *cause* of my pain and suffering — my choice for the ego. When I'm in a "higher" vibration it feels better and I'm calmer. However, it's still a separated state because "I" as Jackie am in it.

A Course in Miracles helps us go all the way home. Observing our thoughts without judgment and letting them be transformed and released will bring us peace of mind. We cannot do this alone.

An important question arises: If it's all an illusion, why does anything matter?

Jesus assures us that it does matter what we do here, meaning, which teacher do I want to follow in the dream? Why stay in the suffering called for in the ego's script? The Course is not asking us to deny our experience here as a body. Jesus says:

> **The body is merely part of your experience in the physical world. Its abilities can be and frequently are over evaluated. However, it is almost impossible to deny its existence in this world. Those who do so are engaging in a particularly unworthy form of denial.[7]**

Because we believe in the world and the body, Jesus first helps us change our interpretation of them. We learn how to use the body lovingly, which means we will let the Holy Spirit be our guide. This has been so helpful. This is how I start my day — putting the Holy Spirit in charge. This is how we start to undo the false self. Even though the world is illusory, it is not at all helpful to stop there and think nothing matters. Since we believe we're here, Jesus slowly helps us transform our thinking. There is hope!

Before we can let our bodies go, we first have to change their purpose — the body in and of itself is neutral and only responds to the intentions of the mind. We learn to see shared interests instead of separate interests. We all share the same mind. Also, we learn to forgive instead of judge and attack. When do we do this? Whenever anything bothers us. Whenever we are disappointed because whatever we rely upon in the world has failed — this is when we're motivated to find another way!

My life under the Holy Spirit's direction becomes my classroom where He uses all the scenarios that have been scripted out for me as forgiveness opportunities. Ken Wapnick explains this well:

> Most importantly, people should never deny what seems to be happening to them in their dreams, for these events become the means of helping them to awaken from the dream. Rather, they should pay careful attention to such experiences and *then* ask the Holy Spirit for help in becoming a happy learner, and accepting His happy dreams of correction to replace the nightmare dreams that their egos had made.[8]

Our mind's belief in the false self, the ego, is the one and only problem. We must keep going back to this basic premise or else we stay on the merry-go-round. Many New Age approaches ultimately won't work because the mind is left unhealed.

Why Many New Age Approaches Keep Us Stuck!

Many of the world's methods will work temporarily, but then we're back to fear again. I've tried many of them, with temporary success. I'm grateful for them. However, I was left unsatisfied because worry and fear always returned. Would I ever be free of this? We cannot escape from fear without undoing its *cause*, and this is unconscious to us. No matter how noble our efforts are, if the cause is overlooked, we will remain stuck. True healing does not occur by changing anything in the dream; in the illusion.

Many New Age approaches, while beneficial and can be used to help you feel better temporarily, do not even know about the unconscious guilt buried in the mind that needs to be undone. Many paths are focused on having a better life here, not even knowing it's a dream. This is why many approaches will only get you so far. Their goal is to fix illusions from within the illusion. Or, they know the world is a dream or illusion, but think that you have to make the world a happier place *first* and then you can awaken. Or, they teach that you have to give something up in order to be "spiritual" and worthy — the path of asceticism for example. Lastly, some approaches believe only our fears and the bad stuff are illusory, or only the ego is illusory and that once we let go of fear in favor of love, we will be healed and live well as a body or soul or some other form that is *separate* from our Source.

Some approaches have you connect with the "larger" part of who you are. This can be a very helpful stepping stone, but stops short if the focus keeps reinforcing the idea that there's a *you* that's real as an individual, and that you will graduate to a higher level of *you*, still separate from your Source. If the idea that we're not separate is not addressed and forgiven, the Course teaches that we cannot undo our unconscious guilt that gave rise to the false self.

Incidentally, ACIM is certainly not the only path to awakening — it says that it is one of many thousands —

but it can be said that it is one of the quicker paths. The aforementioned examples serve the purpose of pointing out how the Course is unique in its teachings. It is never about fixing up a non-existent world, but helping you wake up from your dream that there *is* a world. It's directing us how to change the thought that gave *rise* to the world. Again, this is not a small distinction. ACIM is not against you having a better life here; in fact, my life has improved, especially how I *experience* it. However, the Course reminds us that what we really want — perfect inner peace, security love, joy and happiness — will not ultimately be found in anything external.

Changing the Purpose of Our Relationships

As a body in the world we look around for people to meet our needs, what the Course calls our "special love" and "special hate" relationships. Our needs may get met in one moment, but not in the next. This purpose for our relationships does not work because it's based on a false belief about ourselves; that we are separate from God and have all kinds of lack which has to be fulfilled by people and objects external to us.

> **A sense of separation from God is the only lack you really need correct.**[9]

This is where *purpose* comes in. If we don't like what we are feeling, we can change its purpose; we can change our mind. We don't need to continue to believe in the thought system taught by the ego. The ego does not want us to remember God's perfect love. To the ego, only our external special relationships are important. It tells us that what is out there will bring us happiness; that is our reality. Furthermore, the ego teaches that we can only be happy here at the expense of another. One of the ego's major principles is one or the other.

Let's use my husband Mark again as an example. I know that the script is written, so any disagreement with Mark is already there. However, how I *experience* the interaction is up to me. Will I feel my position is attacked so I have to attack back (ego)? Or will I recognize that this is my dream and I have the power to choose how I see it (Holy Spirit).

It's incredibly freeing to be in the right mind because that awareness allows me to acknowledge that bodies often disagree and I can state my opinion without any need to convince him I'm right. My happiness and peace are no longer dependent on his behavior, his acceptance of me, or in a particular outcome "I" deem as the right one. This has been such an interesting change for me over the years. My purpose for my relationships has changed.

Remember to be light about it. We take everything so seriously here! Just what the ego wants because that's what we did in the beginning — we took the "tiny mad idea" of separation seriously. What does that mean? It means it produced "effects." Remember what the effects are? The whole world we see.

As we practice the Course, we learn to withdraw our belief in the ego's interpretation of our lives, namely, that we can only be happy by manipulating situations outside of ourselves. We recognize that our bodies are part of the projection, and I can choose a different teacher for the interpretation of what is happening around me. We don't deny our experiences and we don't deny that we are experiencing a world out there. We have already made it real; we don't deny it. The Course says that is an unworthy form of denial. Rather we deny the ego's interpretation of the world, or in other words, we withdraw our belief in its interpretation. This is the shift.

When we begin the day with the teacher of love in our minds, we are released from the burden of judgment. We will never again see things as we did before. With practice, we can learn to be the observer with spiritual sight. Spiritual sight (Vision) actually refers to what we are thinking. When we put the Holy Spirit in charge of our minds, we are reflecting the content of love and connecting to the love throughout the Sonship.

We discover the joyous fact that listening to the right internal teacher brings us freedom from anxiety, depression, discouragement and needless suffering. Not overnight, because this is a process involving changing long-standing habits, but you will notice some changes immediately. You will notice that you are reacting less and stopping yourself to switch to thinking with the Holy Spirit. This doesn't mean that you stop addressing your issues. It does mean that with Jesus in your mind, guiding you instead of the ego, you are being well-taught. Remembering these ingredients for inner peace is how the Course becomes practical in my life.

Just recognize in your moments of darkness that a part of your mind chose this on another level. Not on this level of the world where you believe you are. There's no need to feel guilty about what happens because it's not who you *really* are. You are watching a movie and you are the star of it. You're also the director and producer. You can watch a different script of your movie — the forgiveness script. *What* has been scripted out may or may not change, but your *experience* of the events will. That's the Holy Spirit's correction of the ego's script of sin, guilt and fear. You can get to the point where it doesn't matter what happens in your dream because you know it's a dream. Coming from this awareness you will only be helpful to yourself and others. You won't even have to decide what your helpfulness will look like. I cannot begin to describe how freeing that is.

So the key to living in this world is to change your internal teacher if you are not at peace, which then changes your *interpretation* of the world and removes the obstacles to the awareness of love, "which is your natural inheritance."

Mind is key. When you change your mind, you are allowing healing to take place.

You are joining with God in healing the symbolic contents of the split mind. You carry this attitude into the world, into all situations and all relationships. This is our function here.

I wanted to remove conflict from my mind. I wanted to know why the world is the way it is. The keys to living in this world, which I've shared, have changed my life dramatically over the last 15 years. The purpose of my life has changed. I still perform my many roles, but I do so peacefully and with true forgiveness as my guiding light.

CHAPTER 9

Putting the Pieces Back Together

> Row, row, row your boat, gently down the stream. Merrily, merrily, merrily, merrily, life is but a dream. — English Nursery Rhyme

We are bound to judgment here in the world. We cannot escape without help. We don't necessarily need to change our roles, careers, or relationships, just our inner teacher. If the other things happen to change, so be it. What matters is that our peace, after having made the choice for Jesus or the Holy Spirit, will direct all our functioning here. Before you make any decisions, try to shift your inner teacher and, if you can, wait until fear or confusion subsides. What happens will be the best for all concerned. Your focus is only on the love in your mind.

> **How can God's Son awaken from the dream? It is a dream of judgment. So he must judge not, and he will awaken.[1]**

Remember, the ego's meaning of judgment in the Course is condemnation. We separate people here in dreamland into those to be hated and those to be loved. Why would we condemn our dream figures? They've done nothing to us in reality. After all, we put them there in order to see our perceived guilt in them and not ourselves. Without our judgments we would cease to exist, the ego tells us. This is why it's extremely difficult to give them up! Judgment is always based on the past according to the ego. The Holy Spirit's Vision can replace the ego's judgment by seeing people, in the present, as either expressing love or calling out for it.

I leave you with these "reminders" as we conclude our time together for now.

- Be kind and gentle with yourself, others, and with your spiritual practice. *You can believe what you made yourself to be or wake up to what God would have you be.*

- Remember to smile more frequently and remember to laugh! This is not laughing at people, but at the thought that we could really make up all this strife! We forgot to laugh seemingly long ago at the "tiny mad idea" that we could be anything less than perfect Spirit. Each moment we have a grievance, we now have two ways of looking at it.

- How do we live here in the world? Merrily, gently and kindly. We let the Holy Spirit be our guide instead of the ego.

There is a place in you where there is perfect peace. There is a place in you where nothing is impossible. There is a place in you where the strength of God abides.[2]

- The "you" *A Course in Miracles* is addressing is you as *mind*, not as a body. Focus on the memory of love in your mind and all the pieces of your life will take care of themselves.

- An illusion is an illusion is an illusion. There is no hierarchy of illusions because they're all untrue. That is why:

There's no order of difficulty in miracles. One is not "harder" or "bigger" than another.[3]

The above statement could say that there's no order of difficulty in solving problems. This is because the Course is teaching that there is only one problem — our belief in separation from our Source. All the problems in the world are projections of that one illusory thought. A miracle is the shift in perception that sees illusion and contrasts it with truth.

A miracle is a correction. It does not create, nor really change at all. It merely looks on

> **devastation, and reminds the mind that what it sees is false.**[4]

- Positive thinking will only get you so far when you're positively thinking there's a world outside of you!

Merely switching negative thoughts to positive ones is not looking at them and forgiving them. Although it is helpful temporarily, it won't undo the unconscious guilt that's necessary for inner peace and eventually, enlightenment. Enlightenment according to the Course is awakening from the dream of separation to our true reality as perfect oneness with God.

> **Enlightenment is but a recognition, not a change at all.**[5]

Recognition of the light within us is not a change because there's nothing to change *from*; the separation has not occurred.

How do I live *in* the world knowing I'm not *of* it? For me it's all about remembering...

Remember my friends...there is a place inside us where there is perfect peace. In the quiet stillness of our mind, we can hear the Holy Spirit's Voice reminding us when we experience suffering of any kind to look at the world from His perspective. He reminds us that the world is not being done *to* us, it is being done *by* us. We are not victims of the world we see. When we change our mind we have a different purpose for, and *experience* of the world. We are at cause. *Do you remember?*

Any consistent peace requires willingness to question the false idols we've made to replace our Oneness in a realm we've never really separated from — our true home in Heaven. *Do you remember?*

Looking at people and circumstances without judgment, but with the gentle guidance of the Holy Spirit or Jesus, shifts our belief from illusions to Truth. We start to wake up and experience inner peace. Inner peace is the condition of the Kingdom of Heaven. *Do you remember?*

The ego — the false idea in the mind projecting the world including seeming individuals - wants what it made to be real, so we're up against its shrieking voice! The ego speaks first and loudest only because we've given it the power to do so. The Holy Spirit's Voice is always there patiently awaiting our return when we're ready to give up our dream of specialness and duality. *Do you remember?*

Withdraw belief in the false you and the real you will reveal itself.

A Course in Miracles says **"Forgiveness...is still and quietly does nothing....It merely looks, and waits, and judges not."**[6] Why? Because there's nothing to do in a projection. The world is a projection coming from the mind that made it as a substitute for our real life in Heaven. We believe the projection is real only when we identify with the ego. What does forgiveness wait for? For us to change our mind. *Do you remember?*

We can be part of the solution, stress free and at peace in each moment by not indulging the ego's script of sin, guilt & fear. We can elect instead to correct our perception each time we're about to judge (condemn) someone or something. We stop and think with the Holy Spirit before saying or doing anything. This is how we help heal the entire Sonship. This is done in the mind — indeed our change of mind heals. When we choose the miracle, we make that choice for everyone because all minds are joined, being that there's really only one. That choice will direct all our functioning and inform all our decisions in the world. *Remember this with me.*

* * *

A Course in Miracles has answered every question I've ever had. I know why I was often joyful growing up for no apparent reason. It didn't have anything to do with what was happening in the world. It was *internal.* Nowadays the "I", as Jackie, is no longer in the forefront of my experience, and I can live with the peaceful purpose of awakening from the dream of separation. I continue to practice every day.

I'm grateful to have clarification on why, throughout my life, I was hearing the gentle reminder "everything will be okay". Indeed, it *is* okay and always was. Not in dreamland, but in Reality.

My wish for you is a life filled with miracles. You can be *in* the world, but not *of* it. You can navigate the dream with your right-minded teacher. You will awaken when the time is right. In reality you're already there. There isn't anywhere else. There is no hurry. For now, allow the love and joy of What you really are to flow through your mind being the content through which your talents, words and actions are expressed in "the world." *A Course in Miracles* is not important, the love behind it is.

These days I'm peaceful and filled with gratitude. You can be too. Not because our lives will be perfect, but because our forgiveness can be. Just keep practicing and know you are loved and not alone. That will make all the difference.

End Notes

All quotes used from *A Course in Miracles* are from the Third Edition, published in 2007. They are used with permission from the copyright holder and publisher, the Foundation for Inner Peace, P.O. Box 598, Mill Valley, CA 94942-0598, www.acim.org and info@acim.org.

In the following notes, please follow the examples below to correlate the References to the numbering system used in *A Course in Miracles*.

T-11.V.13:1. = Text, Chapter 11, Section V, Paragraph 13, Sentence 1.

W-pI.194.7:1-5. = Workbook, Part I, Lesson 194, Paragraph 7, Sentences 1-5.

M-20.4:8. = Manual, Question 20, Paragraph 4, Sentence 8.

S-1.I.3:1-3. = Song of Prayer, Chapter 1, Section 1, Paragraph 3, Sentences 1-3.

Introduction
1. T-10.I.2:1. 2. W-pI.132.6:2-3.

1: How Did We Get Here?
1. Preface, p.xi 2. Karen Casey, *Daily Meditations for Practicing The Course* (Center City, Minnesota: Hazelden, 1995), May 21. 3. T-10.I.2:3-4. 4. T-13.VII.17:6-7. 5. T-20.VIII.7:3-6. 6. T-20.VIII.8:1-2. 7. T-4.I.9:1-2. 8. T-27.VIII.6:2. 9. M-24.6:4-7. 10. W.pI.160. 11. T-14.II.2:4. 12. W-pI.132.5:3. 13. T-21.in.1:7. 14. T-27.VII.7:4. 15. T-27.VII.13:4.

2: Why Is the World Insane?
1. W.pII.3.1:1-4. 2. T-1.VI.2:1-2. 3. T-20.VII.6:2-6. 4. Kenneth Wapnick, *Glossary-Index for A Course in Miracles 6th Edition*

(Temecula, California: Foundation for *A Course in Miracles,* 2006), 181. 5. T-9.VII.6:1-4.

3: True Forgiveness and the Miracle

1. W-pII.1.1:1-4. 2. T-23.II.19:1-3. 3. T-2.V.A.16(6). 4. Wapnick, *Glossary-Index for A Course in Miracles 6th Edition,* 32. 5. W-pII.13.3:1. 6. W-pII.13.1:1-4. 7. T-1.I.1:1-4. 8. T-2.I.5:6. 9. T-22.III.6:7. 10. T-19.IV.D.12:7-8. 11. W-pI.161.3:1-3. 12. W-pI.16.3:4. 13. 13. Gary Renard, *The Disappearance of the Universe* (Carlsbad, California: Hay House, 2002), 238. 14. Preface, p.ix. 15. T-8.III.4:2. 16. Wapnick, *Glossary-Index for A Course in Miracles 6th Edition,* 112.

4: Our Life Scripts Are Written

1. W-pI.158.4:5. 2. W-pI.158.4:1-5. 3. Kenneth Wapnick, *The Message of A Course in Miracles Volume One: All Are Called 2nd Edition* (Temecula, California: Foundation for *A Course in Miracles,* 2007), 72-73. 4. Kenneth Wapnick, *A Vast Illusion: Time According to A Course in Miracles 3rd Edition* (Temecula, California: Foundation for *A Course in Miracles,* 2006), 10. 5. W-pI.23.2:3-7. 6. M-20.4:8.

5: If the World's an Illusion, What Is My Purpose Here?

1. T-23.IV.4:7, 5:1-3. 2. T-11.V.13:1. 3. W-pI.194.7:1-5. 4. S-1.I.3:1-3. 5. T-30.IV.5:1-3. 6. T-2.IV.5:1-6

6: Relationships

1. T-15.V.4:1-2. 2. Wapnick, *Glossary-Index for A Course in Miracles 6th Edition,* 196. 3. T-26.X.4:1. 4. T-19.IV.C.11:8-10. 5. M-20.4:8

7: Who Is the Holy Spirit and How Does He Help Us?

1. T-28.IV.8:1-2. 2. T-27.IV.5:3. 3. T-27.IV.1:1. 4. Kenneth Wapnick, *Q&A: Detailed Answers to Student-Generated Questions on the Theory and Practice of A Course in Miracles* (Temecula, California: Foundation for *A Course in Miracles,* 2018), Q#457. 5. W-in.8:1-6. 6. T-21.in.1:7.

8: The Keys to Living in This World

1. T-27.VII.2:1-3. 2. T-27.VIII.10:1-6. 3. T-1.I.1:1-4. 4. W-pI.34. 5. T-in.1:6-7. 6. T-28.II.7:1-4. 7. T-2.IV.3:8-11. 8. Gloria Wapnick and Kenneth Wapnick, *The Most Commonly Asked Questions About A Course in Miracles 2nd Edition* (Temecula, California: Foundation for *A Course in Miracles,* 2003), 49. 9. T-1.VI.2:1.

9: Putting the Pieces Back Together
1. T-29.IX.2:3-5. 2. W-pI.47.7:4-6. 3. T-1.I.1:1-2. 4. W-pII.13.1:1-3. 5. W-pI.188.1:4. 6. W-pII.1.4:1, 3

References

Casey, Karen. *Daily Meditations for Practicing The Course.* Center City, Minnesota: Hazelden Publishing, 1995.

Foundation for Inner Peace. *A Course in Miracles: Combined Volume.* Mill Valley, California: Foundation for Inner Peace, 2007.

Renard, Gary. *The Disappearance of the Universe.* Carlsbad, California: Hay House, 2002.

Wapnick, Gloria and Kenneth Wapnick, Ph.D. *The Most Commonly Asked Questions About A Course in Miracles 2nd Edition.* Temecula, California: Foundation for *A Course in Miracles*, 2003.

Wapnick, Kenneth, Ph.D. *A Vast Illusion: Time According to A Course in Miracles 3rd Edition.* Temecula, California: Foundation for *A Course in Miracles*, 2006.

Wapnick, Kenneth, Ph.D. *Glossary-Index for A Course in Miracles 6th Edition.* Temecula, California: Foundation for *A Course in Miracles*, 2006.

Wapnick, Kenneth, Ph.D. *Q&A: Detailed Answers to Student-Generated Questions on the Theory and Practice of A Course in Miracles.* Temecula, California: Foundation for *A Course in Miracles*, 2018.

Wapnick, Kenneth, Ph.D. *The Message of A Course in Miracles Volume One: All Are Called 2nd Edition.* Temecula, California: Foundation for *A Course in Miracles*, 2007.

ABOUT THE AUTHOR

JACKIE LORA JONES, C.Ht., is a Broadcast Journalist, Certified Clinical Hypnotherapist and Spiritual Counselor. Whether speaking to *A Course in Miracles* groups, her work in the media, or in private counseling sessions, she helps people worldwide transform their lives. Jackie's methods facilitate a connection to inner guidance and the Higher Self, which the Course terms the Holy Spirit or Jesus, enabling a more peaceful & forgiving approach to the issues and challenges of everyday life, leading to the awakened mind and return to Spirit/God/Perfect Oneness.

As a holistic journalist, Jackie focuses on "journalism that heals." Through interviews and stories that inspire and uplift, her goal is to shine a bright light on the power of Spirit within all of us.

Jackie was born in Toledo, Ohio to two professional educators. Her father, Ron Lora (retired) was an award-winning History professor who taught at the University of Toledo. Her mother, Doris Lora (retired) was a Music professor at the University of Toledo before changing careers and receiving her Ph.D. in Psychology. They are active in philanthropic projects, writing, editing and community support.

Jackie has been a student of metaphysics for nearly two decades and has fine-tuned her intrinsic skills in psychotherapy and the power of the mind. Her goal is to help people awaken their minds and discover inner peace. For more, visit her website at jackie.news.

Printed in Great Britain
by Amazon

82043059R00119